Master Adulting

Anxiety and Four Key Factors

© Paul Neumann 2025
All rights reserved.

No part of this book may be reproduced, stored, or transmitted in any form or by any means, electronic, mechanical, photocopying, recording, or otherwise, without the prior written permission of the publisher, except for brief quotations used in reviews or scholarly works. It is illegal to copy this book, post it to a website, or distribute it by any other means without permission.

The author has made every effort to ensure the accuracy of the information presented in this book, but the content is for informational purposes only and should not be construed as professional advice. The publisher and author disclaim any liability for errors, omissions, or for any actions taken based on the information contained herein.

First Edition.

Page layout: Frixos Ioannides

ISBN   978-1-7638429-0-8 (Printed version)
        978-1-7638429-1-5 (Digital version)

Master Adulting

Anxiety and Four Key Factors

Paul Neumann

MELBOURNE 2025

Contents

Acknowledgements 7
About the Author 8
Introduction 10

Chapter 1 – Anxiety **14**
    Fight or Flight 15
    Perception 24
    Anxiety's Influence 26
    The Anxiety Foundation 27
    Variation in Anxiety levels 33
    The Counter to Anxiety 37
    The Confidence Analogy 40
    Elements of Anxiety 46
    The Role of Achievement 51
    Building Confidence 53
    Understanding Our Environments 54
    The Four Common Factors 57

Chapter 2 – Factor 1: Introducing Blame and Responsibility . . **58**
    The Role of Responsibility in Conflict 59
    Barriers to Taking Responsibility 69
    The Training of Responsibility 71
    Training Irresponsibility 74
    Failing to Teach 74
    Actively Teaching Irresponsibility 75
    Learning by Experience 76
    The Pleasure of Irresponsibility 77
    The Takeaway 81

Chapter 3 - Foundations of the Blame and
Responsibility Dynamic **83**
    The Child–Adult Perspective 83

Chapter 4 – Blame and Responsibility:
The Next Level **91**
    The Blamer 94
    The Responsible 95
    The Self-blamer 96
    The Avoider 109
    Identification Considerations 112
    The Overly Responsible 114

The Takeaway	118
The Narcissistic Partner	118
The Narcissistic Parent	119
What Influences Which Strategy We Take?	120
Blame and Responsibility in "Positive" Scenarios	122
The Takeaway	123

Chapter 5 – Addressing Responsibility ... 128
How to Build Responsibility	128
Rewarded Irresponsibility	135
How to Take Responsibility for Yourself	137
The Gains of Taking Responsibility	142
Ramifications of Blame and Responsibility	147
The Takeaway	148

Chapter 6 – Factor 2: The Primary Pitfall ... 151
No Pitfall: Correct Assumption and the Same Spirit of Intent	159
Clear Pitfall: Projection and Misidentifying the Spirit of Intent	160
Blindside Pitfall: Failing to Identify the Spirit of Intent	168
Commonality of the Pitfall	170
Anxiety and the Primary Pitfall	171
Avoiding the Primary Pitfall	172
The Takeaway	174
Disclaimer	175

Chapter 7 – Factor 3: Know the Cost ... 176
The Importance of Considered Decision-Making	179
Getting Better at Knowing the Costs	181
Conscious Decision-making	191
The Takeaway	191

Chapter 8 – Factor 4: The Take-home Message ... 192
Encoding Our Take-home Message	192
Internal Influence on Encoding	193
Directing Your Own Mindset	197
Is All Bias Unhelpful?	199
External Influences on Encoding	202
The Importance of Early Encoding	206
What We Forgot to Encode	210
Memory Encoding vs Internal Dialogue	214
Bringing it all Together	216
The Takeaway	223
Final Thoughts	224

Acknowledgements

First and foremost I'd like to thank God for providing me with all the tools needed to make this book happen. Any wisdom or insights that may come from this work are due only to his having gifted me the ability to discover and produce them. As a person who has never enjoyed or sought to write anything, I can't help but think it was his influence that had me wanting, and enjoying the process of putting this work together. Equally, I am grateful for his having created a period in my life that afforded me the time and space to dedicate to this work. I'd also like to thank all the clients I've seen over the years, each of which inched me closer and closer to seeing how Anxiety and these four factors develop and present within us.

Thank you to my Students and Supervisees, who first made the suggestion that I write down some of the core and common concepts that I have come across in my practice. Thank you also to those friends who helped keep me motivated to finish, and publish this work. Their blind enthusiasm towards reading my work once it was done was very encouraging, motivating, and terrifying. Thank you all, I hope this doesn't disappoint. Finally, thank you to the reader, for without you the purpose of this book can not be fulfilled. I appreciate the time you have taken to read and consider some of what life has taught me about us.

May the content of this work be taken in the spirit it was intended, that of understanding, acceptance, and growth.

About the Author

Having dipped my toe into studying Computer Science and then Engineering, I settled on finishing my Bachelor of Science, and then Masters of Clinical Psychology. This lead to starting clinical practice in 2009, followed by taking on supervision of students a few years later.

Those who know me have accused me of being efficient, logical, and, at times, somewhat off-center when it comes to perspectives on things. I was always skeptical about this appraisal by others; I never felt any more logical or efficient than anyone else, and certainly less so than some I've come across. But when you get told something for decades, there may be something to it, and listening never hurt anyone. I hope that the efficient and logical traits have helped me in my work. As for the third, well, I'm not sure if that's a virtue or a polite way of saying "strange", but in any case, I have always tended to speak my mind and not shy away from exploring an idea. Unfortunately, this has had a mixed response from others, from bewilderment and rejection to gratitude or valuable insight. My hope for this book is that I can convey things in such a way that offers more of the latter than the former.

My understanding and approach to psychology are largely influenced by the likes of Carl Jung, Carl Rogers, and Albert Ellis, to name a few. I do not claim to be an expert in any of their works, but rather, their perspectives have tended to strike a chord with my own thinking, and likely influenced it. Also influencing my thinking is my general desire to understand intricate or complex mechanisms, which is perhaps the common thread with my earlier ventures into areas such as IT and engineering.

I approach my work with the mindset that all people are capable of the entire range of human nature, from good to evil, selfishness to selflessness, greed to generosity, and all spaces in between. That each person tends to work within a narrower range of the full spectrum of human nature, deviating only when life circumstances force them to, and even then, there is no guarantee of a shift.

I believe that people have a choice in everything they do, even when they do not realize they are making a choice, or if they do not see it. Importantly, I believe that with exploration, education, and empowerment of choice, people can choose to improve their circumstances or choose not to. The extent or ease with which they do this will vary greatly, but as a psychologist, I struggle to believe we do not exercise some influence over our thoughts and choices. My hope for this book is that it can be of help to someone who is looking to better understand themselves and subsequently make improved and positive (but likely difficult) changes for themselves and their lives, as well as those around them.

Introduction

Everyone seems to have an opinion on how to raise children, but what if that goes wrong? If your upbringing was less than ideal and contributed to your current issues, learning how to raise a child doesn't help you. What you need is to learn how to raise an adult. How do you take what you have today and develop that into what will serve you better tomorrow? This book aims to give you a clear and practical approach to doing just that. It will highlight and explore four common patterns in one's psychology that can not only improve your functioning as an adult but also help to undo some of the problematic teachings of your childhood. Besides, who wants to raise a "child," shouldn't we always be seeking to raise an adult? Care and nurture a child, absolutely, but let's start raising adults.

After 15 years of practice as a clinical psychologist and supervisor, I've found a number of reoccurring patterns that present themselves in clients, students, supervisees, and people in general. I say patterns, but it's more of an underlying set of processes, or dynamics, playing out in a person's thoughts, actions, or general understanding. An underlying, often unconscious process that drives or informs a person's thoughts and actions, which, over time, leads to certain life outcomes.

For simplicity, I refer to this pattern of underlying processes or dynamics as "factors." In my experience, these common factors often underlie all the issues that people face. In most cases, people don't seem to be aware of them. People tend to think they are consciously making life choices or that they are in control of how or what they think. They tend not to assume there is some underlying, unconscious drive or factor that is contributing to if not entirely dominating their decision-making. Over time, these factors are steering their life direction one decision (or non-decision) at a time. Often, when these factors are made clear and addressed, things start to resolve, and people can exercise more conscious awareness and, therefore, decision-making. This is not to say that every issue in that person's life resolves; however, it provides an understanding of their situation and provides them with the insight they need to make the changes they want to make.

I make no assertion that I am the first to identify these factors or even write about them. But in my experience, there seems to be a lack of attention given to them. In fact, of all the professional conversations I've had throughout my 15 years of clinical practice and six years of formal education, I cannot recall any significant time given to these factors. Most professional conversations I have experienced relate to modes of therapy and associated theory, diagnosis, assessment, and client engagement—all of which are critical components of good therapeutic work. However, it misses a significant component of human psychological development in understanding clients and helping them understand themselves.

As a supervisor who has worked with both students and registered psychologists, I was often surprised to hear my supervisees mention they had little knowledge about the factors I will explore in this book, or that they paid them little attention in their work. Often, their approach to working with a client was to formally assess, diagnose, and apply evidence-based therapy for that diagnosis. This process is, of course, a sound one. However, it doesn't necessarily require the therapist to "understand" the person but simply to "assess, diagnose, and apply a template." I have found that both a person's engagement and quality of outcomes are often tied to how well they come to understand themselves, as well as feeling thoroughly understood by their treating psychologist.

I wrote this book as an introduction to some of these common factors, which I believe are often at the core (or near to it) of many common presentations and general human development. I believe that when understood and explored, they can lead people onto the path of recovery. It also helps to empower them to continue that path with less need for ongoing sessions with a therapist. An analogy for this is a damaged car. Taking it to a panel beater will repair the cosmetic damage and get you back on the road. However, if the driver doesn't improve their skills, they'll soon be back at the panel beater, but this time with less money and less confidence in their ability to drive. What this person needs is a driving instructor, someone to help them learn the skills to prevent future accidents and damage. Similarly, a *therapist* can help repair the damage in your life, while a *psychologist* can teach you how to prevent causing further damage. This analogy betrays one of my underlying views, that there is a difference between a therapist and a psychologist. In my experience, there seems to be a greater shift towards training therapists who can "get you back on the road" as opposed to psychologists who take the time to broaden one's understanding of self. Perhaps it's a sign of our current society's values or needs. I believe the best path is to focus on the driving force rather than the surface damage. Otherwise, "Teach a man to fish, and they can feed themselves for a lifetime."

This book is not a handbook for a new (or even old) therapy method. It is simply a reminder of some underlying mechanisms that drive us, which can steer us in the wrong direction unless we take the wheel. Anyone can benefit from this "reminder." An everyday person can empower themselves, and therapists can know what to watch for in their clients to understand them better and provide improved service. Much like psychodynamic or psychoanalytic approaches, I believe that if we can shine a light on these underlying factors, then people can be more consciously aware of what and why they are doing or thinking as they are. From there, they can now make informed decisions as to what they want to do next, as opposed to being driven by this underlying, invisible force or unconscious factor. In my view, this is the first step to conscious decision-making, as ultimately, if we are aware of the principles/factors and emotions pushing and pulling on our decision-making, then we can make an informed, active decision on how to proceed. Assuming, that is, that the person is willing to act against these underlying desires, fears, and instincts.

I aim to provide, in simple language, a fundamental understanding of what drives many common issues in people's lives. My hope is that by developing an understanding of these underlying mechanisms, people can identify them in themselves and others. For trained professionals, it can help augment their work and provide a greater understanding of human psychology and treatment. In the case of the everyday person, it can help you be more aware of your own processes and empower you to actively choose your own path, to help you develop and grow by paying attention to yourself and your choices.

The four factors I will address relate to a certain facet of human development. These factors often operate unconsciously, meaning they influence our behavior without our conscious awareness. They are:

1. The Blame-Responsibility Dynamic (Personal Development and Relationships)
2. The Primary Pitfall (Awareness and Interpersonal Understanding)
3. Knowing the Cost (Decision Making)
4. The Take-home Message (Learning Bias and Attitude Development)

It is important to note that underlying all these factors is the very important issue of *anxiety*. I would argue that anxiety has a strong influence on these factors and, indeed, on all of our actions, thoughts, and development. I would go as far as to say that anxiety is the foundation upon which these four factors, and many others, are built. So, it is vital to have a solid understanding of how anxiety works when it is at play and how it has developed over one's life. As such, I will provide a framework for understanding anxiety before delving into the details of these four factors.

Chapter 1 – Anxiety

In this chapter, I will aim to provide an overview of how anxiety plays a role in the key dynamics of later chapters. For those who are well versed in anxiety, in how it is triggered, why it is triggered, and what short- and long-term effects it can have, this chapter may not offer much in the way of technical knowledge. However, I hope it can offer a different perspective on how to view it in clients and as a phenomenon in itself. For those who have never delved into understanding anxiety, this chapter should provide a strong basis from which to understand and view it.

The four factors become clearer when we understand one fundamental idea: our brain's primary role is to keep us alive. While some may argue that the brain's primary role is to think, create, control the body, or perhaps pursue spirituality, none of these functions occur in a corpse.

So, if we accept that the brain's primary role is survival, then anxiety can be seen as the CEO of that role. Anxiety has the power to shut down or hijack the rest of your brain to maximize your chances of survival. It will simply step in and take over whenever it sees fit; it will not consult you, it will not hesitate, it will simply fly into action.

Anxiety, often referred to as the *fight or flight* response, is designed to react nearly instantly for the very reason of getting you out of danger or keeping you alive. When you catch what looks like a danger out of the corner of your eye (a snake, a bear, a ninja), your body reacts quickly and without further thought. The signal of potential danger is sent directly from the brain stem, down the spine, and into action. It does not send a signal to the front of your brain to ask if you want to respond or not, nor does it send a signal to your long-term memory on how to identify different species of bears or snakes. That would all take time, which prolongs your reaction time and increases the chance of injury or death. Essentially, the anxiety sector is overriding or short-cutting the system. It has the power to make your body react without your input! It is instinct or *reaction* at this point. It steps in and takes charge without caring what you want, and you are powerless to do anything about it—at least until it decides to hand back control. I would argue that any system with that level of authority over the brain and body is there for a good reason—to ensure your survival. Therein lies my case for the brain's primary purpose being to keep you alive.

Keep it simple: The brain's primary role is to keep you alive. A dead person paints no pictures, shows no kindness, nor solves any problem. Only once your brain is convinced of its survival will it shift to other processes. Before all else, survive.

The common understanding about anxiety is that it is bad, unhelpful, or to be feared; however, it can often be very helpful, not just for your immediate survival, but also as an indicator or driver for acting on something that is not an imminent danger.

Fight or Flight

The fight or flight response seems to be a commonly understood phenomenon, or at least widely heard of. It is a general descriptor of the "anxiety" response. When we become anxious, we tend to either prepare for a fight to survive a threat or run away (flight) to avoid a threat. In truth, there is a third option, "freeze," where we become almost parallelized with fear and cease all movement (freeze) or ability to problem solve out of a situation we ordinarily would not struggle with. But given that this freeze response is less common than the other two, we commonly refer to this anxiety response as the fight or flight response.

So, what actually happens when this anxiety response is triggered? In simple terms:
1. You perceive a threat, whether real or imagined.
2. Your brain instinctively reacts to this perceived threat.
3. Certain chemicals such as cortisol and adrenaline are released into your bloodstream.
4. These chemicals have a significant impact on your body and brain.
5. You interpret this psychological response as feeling anxious.

And in an unhelpful spiral of anxiety:

6. You begin to panic, sensing something is wrong and reinforcing the perception of a threat.
7. Your body responds by releasing even more chemicals, which intensifies the anxiety symptoms.
8. The escalation may lead to a panic attack and a heightened fear of experiencing anxiety.

The above is a simplified breakdown of the usual process. If that's all you take from this chapter, that's just fine; it may be all you need to tackle anxiety on your own. But knowing a little more about some of the key points will help uncover what's really happening and likely help you overcome it. So, let's break down some of the key points.

Point 1

As mentioned earlier, this is the stage where our senses identify something that is interpreted as threatening, be it physical, emotional, social, or, in fact, anything that can have a lasting negative impact. This can even occur without you being consciously or at least acutely aware of it.

Point 2

The brain reacts instinctively. We won't be going into the depths of neurology or biology here, but we can expand this point slightly to help provide a basic understanding. In broad terms, the brain is divided into several sections:
1. Frontal lobe: Primarily responsible for executive functions such as planning, decision-making, and considering multiple factors.

2. Temporal lobe: Located on the sides of the brain, involved in memory storage and retrieval, as well as processing auditory information.
3. Occipital lobe: Found at the rear of the brain, processes visual input received from the eyes.
4. Brain stem: Situated at the top of the spine and the base of the brain, responsible for basic functions like motor control and the body's response to threats. It's considered the most primitive part of the brain, focused on survival rather than complex cognitive tasks.

The brain stem, which includes various sub-sections, plays a crucial role in the anxiety response. However, for the sake of clarity and simplicity, we won't delve into its detailed neurology here.

When you perceive some non-threatening day-to-day object, such as a chair, your brain instinctively understands that a chair is not a threat. You likely learned this as a child as you explored your world. However, when we detect a threat, such as a ravenous bear, a snake, or some human threat, our brain will react without thought. It's as though a part of the brain is hard-wired to detect a threat and respond without hesitation. Even that jump scare you experience when watching a movie illustrates your brain's swift response mechanism. Initially, your brain stem detects a potential threat and initiates the fight-or-flight response, preparing your body to react instantly. This primal reaction happens almost instinctively, without consulting your conscious brain. The brain stem is located at the top of your spinal cord and has direct access to the nerves connecting your brain to your entire body, enabling rapid response actions to ensure survival.

In this process, the brain stem prioritizes immediate action over rational thought or planning, which could delay response time and pose a risk in critical situations. It autonomously decides on actions based on survival instincts until it perceives the threat as no longer imminent, at which point control may return to your rational, conscious brain. In truth, we should be thankful for that brain stem; it kept your ancestors alive and is likely why you exist today.

Point 3

Chemical release. Again, this will not be a biochemistry lesson, but it will be a breakdown of two chemicals that your brain releases during this anxiety response. These two chemicals, or more specifically, hormones, are adrenaline and cortisol.

Point 4

Adrenaline is commonly associated with something positive: the "adrenaline" rush. This is true for some but not for others; not everyone likes the feeling of an adrenaline rush. In any case, adrenaline is released in both "exciting" and threatening situations. So, what does it do? In short, adrenaline directly affects the body; its release into the bloodstream triggers the heart to increase its pumping rate. There are several other effects of adrenaline, all of which are associated with essentially boosting the body's ability to fight or flee. Ultimately, the goal is to get maximal oxygen and, therefore, function in the muscles in the body to allow it to protect itself in some way. With blood and, therefore, fuel filling the muscles, we maximize our physical ability to stay alive.

This, of course, has some side effects, including increasing our breathing rate, often rapid or shallow breathing, as well as redirecting levels of blood flow from areas that do not currently improve chances of survival, such as digestion. Blood is redirected from the digestive tract to the limbs to help in this fight-or-flight response. As such, we tend to feel that "sick in the stomach" feeling.

All the commonly known bodily symptoms of anxiety can be attributed to the effects of adrenaline, either directly or indirectly. The shaking hands? That's your body burning off excess adrenaline via twitching your muscles. Something that wouldn't be *as* necessary had you actually run or fought. The increased sweatiness? That's due to the increased body heat from the higher heart rate and blood flow. The tightness in your chest? Well, your heart did just get supercharged; it may well have gone above its normal threshold heart rate for a period of time. And your lungs have also just had a workout. In fact, your entire body has just gone through a stressful event, one that, if triggered

CHAPTER 1 – ANXIETY

appropriately, is a good trade-off of short-term pain/stress for your long-term survival.

What about the other common symptoms of anxiety, things such as poor memory of events or what some refer to as "brain fog." This is where the other hormone, cortisol, comes in. While adrenaline affects the body, cortisol influences the brain (and, to some extent, the body as well). It is commonly known as the "stress" hormone, has many impacts across the body, and plays a role in metabolism, inflammation suppression, blood pressure, and your sleep-wake cycle. But in the case of an anxiety response, it has a more immediate effect on your brain function, as well as the quick release of sugars (glucose) from your liver for fast energy availability.

In the case of an anxiety response, cortisol floods the brain and plays its role in essentially shutting down (or dampening) the parts of the brain that are not immediately required. For example, when faced with a significant threat to your life, you do not need to know what you had planned for next weekend or how to do complex mathematics, so it shuts down or slows these parts of the brain. Equally, you do not need to access your short-term memory, so cortisol helps dull your ability to recall what you had for brunch while you clamber up a tree to escape a pack of rabid hyenas. Be sure to thank cortisol the next time you're in this position.

However, as it's inhibited your short-term memory, it's also not likely to be able to "write" a new memory either, which might be why you don't remember exactly how you ended up in a tree. Some people refer to this as a "Rage blackout." In those instances where someone was so angry (with anger often being a secondary response to fear) during a fight, they claim to have no recollection of what happened. This could be an extreme case of the fight response and the brain shutting down systems to instinctively react to a threat.

More commonly, people who are in the process of an anxiety response, and more so in an actual panic attack, are often observed not to be able to "think straight." They seem to have lost their ability to process information effectively and develop otherwise simple solutions.

This is also seen in someone who is having a trauma response, who is simply reacting to their environment, perhaps having difficulty forming words, and certainly not able to express themselves as they otherwise would. Their ability to communicate is significantly diminished.

When we look at the anxiety response, this makes sense. After all, if your brain is convinced it is under direct threat, its best and ONLY option is to run or fight. And one doesn't need to produce well-considered sentences to do either. So, the next time you see someone who is in the throws of an anxiety attack or having some kind of traumatic flashback/confrontation, keep in mind that person is overwhelmed by hormones/biology and doesn't have access to certain brain functions! It's not their fault they can't communicate or think their way out of a seemingly simple situation. And if it's you who is going through that experience, now you know why you couldn't figure it out or why you can't remember exactly what happened. That covers points three and four. These two hormones, triggered by point two, can temporarily take over the body and brain.

As a community service message here, should you ever see someone seemingly struggling to think straight or communicate as they usually would, consider that they might be having an anxiety attack/trauma response. If they are, I highly recommend you show them warmth and compassion rather than press them for answers or berate them for not making sense. They are likely scared out of their mind and unable to tell you why. They are also likely to be breathing quickly or erratically. I implore you to help them calm themselves; you can do this by reassuring them that they are safe and by helping them regulate their breathing to a steady, slower rate, just as you would if trying to catch your breath after some intense exercise. Give them a few minutes to regulate their breathing and for their body to burn off that adrenaline and cortisol. This will be far more effective than yelling at them to calm down or demanding them to answer you or complete some task. As a bonus, it also helps you to not look reprehensible to any onlookers.

CHAPTER 1 – ANXIETY

Point 5

This point seems self-explanatory, and essentially, it is as it sounds. We experience all the symptoms caused by perceiving a threat, and we experience this as "feeling anxious." However, we often experience this as anxiety because we are usually sitting, standing, or lying down when this process is triggered rather than fighting or fleeing. To make matters worse, we stay in those positions. When this process is triggered, the body's natural response is to run or fight, in other words, to be active. Often, we perceive a threat from giving a speech, going on a date, or meeting with our boss. So, our body starts the anxiety process but isn't allowed to fight or run, and the adrenaline and cortisol circulate the body, and then we wonder what is happening to us. We also don't have the distraction of running or fighting for our lives, so with nothing to occupy our now alert yet compromised mind, we become hyper-focused on what's happening in the body and realize we don't like it!

This can cause us to associate these unpleasant feelings with the person or place where we experienced them, such as our job, a crowd of people, dating, etc. The next time you find yourself at that place, with that person, or at a similar event, you start to expect that unpleasant feeling, which becomes a threat. Congratulations, you have now reached the point of fearing the onset of anxiety itself. This means you are afraid of your own body's survival mechanism, which is there to help you and is always with you.

In essence, you have learned to fear the very thing that can save you from actual danger, the same thing that is likely responsible for keeping your ancestors, and therefore you, alive. Once you start to fear becoming anxious, you are well on your way to developing an anxiety disorder. Perhaps Generalized Anxiety Disorder (GAD), which is essentially when day-to-day things can create anxiety to the point of being overwhelmed, often with seemingly no trigger. You end up almost expecting to be anxious most days, and often, that is what starts the process. More simply, you are prone to becoming anxious to the point of not functioning and not always knowing why.

Points 6–10

Points 6–10 are basically the cycle of anxiety feeding or perpetuating itself. We first experience anxiety, then learn it is unpleasant, so the next time we feel similar symptoms, we start to perceive them as the threat of feeling anxious. This cycles more adrenaline and cortisol, which perpetuates the cycle. Although anxiety can often lead to a very sudden leap into this fight or flight response, there is also a subtle nature to anxiety, one that I feel is often overlooked but is important to highlight.

As mentioned earlier, anxiety is essentially in charge of keeping you alive in a crisis or when there is imminent danger. This is the anxiety that hits us hard and fast, floods our body with adrenaline and cortisol, and triggers the flight or flight response. However, there are also times of milder anxiety: the unease of waking into a tense room, the excitement of reaching a sporting final, and the moment your crush gives you an affirming look.

Let's take the gradual anxiety felt when getting increasingly hungry. At first, your brain simply lets you know you are hungry. If you act on this, everything resolves, if you do not, then over time, you are likely to get irritable and eventually become singularly focused on acquiring food as concentration on other things goes out the window until after eating. This system is designed to provoke feelings of irritation, anger, or similar states in a person when they are hungry, aiming to increase their motivation and capability to obtain food.

This instinct isn't particularly useful when navigating a shopping trolley down the aisles of your local grocery store. However, this system evolved long before the existence of grocery stores—or even buildings, for that matter. It formed when we needed to hunt and kill an animal (often one larger than the hunters themselves) to get that food. When out on a potentially life-threatening hunt, having that anger and desperation that hunger gave you might well be the difference between eating and being eaten.

In this case, your brain and body have decided that creating a hyper-focus on food, due to your extreme hunger, will help you hunt food and survive. At that time, it is less important to be mindful of your manners or considerations of someone else's day, and so we enter that irritable state until our survival is again assured. Essentially, your brain and body are temporarily hijacked to deal with the primary needs first. It will push a primitive drive and desire to assure your safety. It will gently poke and prod at first, but if you fail to respond or cannot, it will take matters into its own hands. It will drug and manipulate you to save you. It has no interest in a democratic vote or moderated discussion. It knows what is needed to ensure its survival and the passing down of its genes, so it will step in when needed. It doesn't care about your sensibilities around kindness to animals or empathetic warmth to your friends and family. Had you acted sooner, you could have preserved those things. But your brain will step in to ensure its survival when push comes to shove. If needed, it will temporarily turn you into an angry, one-eyed monster, or as your brain sees it, an enhanced survival machine!

It is important to distinguish between how we might see what is happening and how our brain may see what it is doing to us. There is no distinction for some people, as these two things align, even in the most desperate situations. In many cases, people feel confused about their emotions, struggle to understand their actions, or experience conflicts between their actions and their thoughts or desires. This branches into many areas of human behavior or psychosocial issues, and although a worthy topic for exploration, for the purpose of survival mechanisms, it suffices to say that it is common for people to be detached from or confused by these processes.

The Takeaway

So why am I highlighting this point? The takeaway is that your brain and body will trigger specific systems to increase your likelihood of survival. You may not see or understand that at the time, but *there is a reason for your actions or reactions*. This applies directly to anxiety but also to more complex issues that may be associated with past traumas or general drives and desires.

Keep it simple: Your brain will trigger anxiety when it feels it needs to in order to survive. You may not be aware or understand why it is being triggered into anxiety, but the unconscious brain has its reasons. Determine what these reasons are, and you will be more likely to be able to control or manage your anxiety.

Perception

One of the key factors to keep in mind when it comes to triggering anxiety is that of the brain having to *perceive* a threat. This perception could be an internal or an external one. External threats are the more obvious things, such as an oncoming car, a dangerous animal, or an armed assailant. An internal perceived threat could be something such as a belief that you will fail at an inconsequential task, a past trauma, or some other past experience or teaching that has you believing you are or will be in danger. These perceptions could be either accurate or inaccurate; however, in either case, anxiety will be triggered all the same.

This is perhaps best illustrated by an example. How many of us have walked a trail and spied what appeared to be a snake/bear/predator in the woods beside us? Your body will instantly flood with adrenaline and recoil from the location where it perceived the threat. Then, you will instinctively do one of two things. Your eyes will home in on what it saw in order to better assess the threat, only to find that the snake is a stick, the bear is a bush, or some other inaccurately perceived threat. Or you'll run down that trail at full *flight* and not look back.

In the instance where you stop and determine the snake was a stick, it could be said that this was a false alarm, and your anxiety was triggered unnecessarily. After all, there was no actual threat. In reality, the brain *perceived* a snake and took over the body momentarily with an instinctual reaction, only to find there was no actual threat from the now-identified stick. However, one could argue that this was still the correct response by the brain. Take the reverse scenario where your brain perceives a stick and does not react. This could result in you continuing to be in close proximity to a danger and, in fact, places you at greater risk of injury or death. In this case, an overreaction is the safer of the two options, and so we could consider this false alarm to be the correct response. "Better safe than sorry."

This same concept tends to hold for those who have an anxiety response to seemingly safe things, such as being in public or giving a speech. Their mind has, however, identified these things as *actual* dangers. Their mind *perceives* these largely safe scenarios as dangerous, likely due to past negative experiences with them. Conversely, an experienced snake catcher will likely have *less* of an anxiety response when facing a snake, likely due to their past experience of how to manage such an encounter.

Keep it simple: Perception of danger is perhaps more important than actual danger, at least in terms of the brain's response to triggering anxiety and attempting to keep us alive or safe.

It is important to note that our anxiety can be triggered by any of our senses but also by our internal beliefs or experiences. We can react to a noise or smell just as much as our vision. We can similarly react to a social, financial, or emotional threat we perceive in our environment. The threat of social embarrassment and, therefore, reduction in social standing is particularly strong in our adolescent years but also well into adulthood. These may not sound like *imminent* dangers, but they are very real ones. Humans are social animals, and we function within social strata or hierarchies that will impact our life opportunities, such as employment/wealth acquisition, group acceptance, and procreation. After all, someone who is socially accepted, liked, and even revered is more likely to acquire more resources, such as friends and money. This may sound strange to some, but even a cursory look at human history will show that a singer, actor, politician, or other public figure will frequently be looked up to by others for no reason other than they appear liked or desirable by the masses. Essentially, if you get the favor of the masses, it can lead to social and financial success.

In a typical "functional" case, this anxiety is only triggered when it is appropriate, short-term, and effective. However, in less functional cases, it can become a significant problem and lead to a range of anxiety disorders. I have worked with many clients who suffer with anxiety. However, not all of them acknowledge or realize the extent of how this anxiety is shaping their decisions, actions, and lives. They have lived with it for so long they assume it is normal; it becomes indistinguishable from their personality and drives their every action. It is those cases that can prove difficult as the anxiety is so ingrained that you must first find a way for them to realize just how pervasive it is. In other cases, it is an acute and distinguishable phenomenon that is more easily identified by all and, therefore, targeted.

Keep it simple: I would argue that it is anxiety that largely sculpts one's decision-making and also has a role to play in things such as personality development and one's ability to attend to and retain information. At times, it does this directly. At other times, it acts as an intermediary influencing the four factors covered in later chapters.

Anxiety's Influence

The overly active perception of threat is the basis of many anxiety disorders. Those who are more anxious tend to perceive threats more often or more intensely than those who are not anxious. This is perhaps the defining feature between someone with problematic anxiety concerns and those whose anxiety is appropriate for the situation.

The overly anxious person will then tend to act in such ways that negatively impact their life. They may believe that taking a trail walk is too dangerous as they may fall or be bitten by a snake, so they opt to never take that walk. However, as a side effect of this attempt to stay safe, they are missing out on exercise, social engagement, and, importantly, the opportunity to recalibrate what they see as dangerous. And so, this person's anxiety starts to perpetuate and build upon itself over time.

Should the anxious person bring themselves to do the trail walk, they may be more focused on scanning for dangers, while their non-anxious walking partner is focused on the beauty of nature. So, while they both walk the same trail, they have different experiences. The anxious person recalls the fear of potential threats rather than a successful and beautiful walk, reinforcing their fears for next time. In contrast, the non-anxious person reinforces their belief that such walks are amazing and has no greater sense of threat or danger associated with them. This is a key element in Factor 4: The Take-home Message.

The Anxiety Foundation

When exploring anxiety as a concept, be it for general understanding or when working through it with a client, I often resort to analogies to explain the concept. The Anxiety Foundation is one such analogy.

Just as our brain has various components built upon one another in order to work as a whole, so too is our mental health (or our psychology), which is built upon core elements in order to function in its entirety. At the base of this healthy functioning is that of our sense of *safety and security*. The greater our sense of safety and security, the lower our sense of anxiety, and the better equipped we are to develop the higher-order parts of our psychology. Let's apply the analogy of a house, where the house represents the individual person. Every house is built upon a foundation, and in this analogy, this foundation consists of our levels of safety, security, and anxiety.

Houses can be built on solid foundations, unsteady, cracked, or unusual foundations, but as long as those foundations are not disturbed in any way that would cause a collapse, the houses can stand just fine. However, should the wind blow, the ground shake, or something otherwise interfere, only the house with strong foundations will remain relatively intact. This analogy holds true for our mental health. Should our psychology be built upon solid foundations, we can withstand difficulties and pressures that push against our *house*. However, if we have weak mental foundations due to reasons such as abuse, neglect, poor guidance, constant negativity, or simply poor teachings, then we are less likely to hold up when the wind blows, when we face a challenge in life, when the earth shakes, or when we come to face our inner fears.

As long as that foundation is secure and not threatened, then the house sits still, and it can be used and built or improved upon. All elements of the brain have an opportunity to function. We can make memories, we can think creatively, we can joke, laugh, and show consideration towards others. As long as the foundation remains secure and stable, we remain functional. However, if this foundation feels threatened, it begins to shake, becoming insecure, and we become less functional.

This threat to the foundation can come from any number of things, from a direct and real threat to your life to the threat of having to speak in public. Anything that causes a person anxiety has the potential to make this foundation shake, and once it starts to shake, everything built on top of it will feel the impact.

The greater the threat (regardless of whether it is real or imagined), the more that house shakes. The walls can start to crack, making them less reliable than they were. Perhaps these walls are your memory, your integrity, your creativity, and your faith. All of these things will suffer and continue to suffer until that foundation (anxiety) is resolved. We need to deal with the anxiety that is within that foundation (deal with the core of your anxiety), or at the very least, deal with what is causing that embedded anxiety to rattle around (remove the immediate trigger for the anxiety). Achieve the former, and you will be extracting the veins of anxiety that run through your foundation. In that way, if the same trigger (life event) presents itself again, there will be no shaking. Achieve the latter, and while your recovery is a welcome one, it only lasts until you encounter that trigger again, albeit with more experience in managing it quickly next time. In any case, quell the anxiety, and the house stabilizes, you return to your normal functioning.

Anyone who has experienced a significant anxiety or panic attack—or been around someone who has—will understand how debilitating this can be and just how much their functioning shuts down during that time. Only when the anxiety has subsided do they start to recover their faculties. During high levels of anxiety, the brain will actively shut down higher-order functions and focus its attention on surviving whatever threat it has identified. From the brain's perspective, those other faculties are not necessary at that moment; all that's needed is the ability to fight or flee to survive the threat. This is why people might not be able to think clearly or even have a clear recollection of the event; their memory sector is partly or entirely shut down. Essentially, your primitive brain is now in charge, and your instincts are calling the shots.

Anxiety, however, is not always a catastrophic earthquake; sometimes, it is just a mild sway or firm breeze. We all experience a degree of anxiety, similar to a boat on the water where there's always some level of movement; the key lies in how much movement there is. Keep in mind that while the house is swaying, it is not at its strongest, even if it still functions. Sometimes, a little swaying is necessary to wake us up and drive us into action. Once it starts to shake, we might find ourselves cowering and paralyzed.

All functions are built atop this Anxiety Foundation, meaning we all have the potential to lose control, be impaired, or be influenced by anxiety. This is something your unconscious mind is already aware of. There's a part of your mind that recognizes the possibility of experiencing this anxiety response at any moment; it's the part of your mind that seeks to avoid this and ensure your safety. This unconscious aspect of your mind likely influences your daily decisions to keep you in a safer space. It's the motivation behind your choice to be polite to the intense, angry man at the bar, the reason you unconsciously smile at everyone to convey friendliness and non-threat, and the driving force behind anything you do to avoid or reduce danger.

All our decisions will have, to one degree or another, considered our safety levels. Even if only unconsciously, our brain will check in with that Anxiety Foundation to see if it feels threatened by something and then decide accordingly. This is not to say that every choice is to avoid a threat or fear. At times, we decide to do something that absolutely induces fear or a threat, but our decision-making process has determined it can manage that level of threat or "shaking of the house." Take, for example, someone bungee jumping or asking someone out on a date. There is a degree of fear or a threat of a negative outcome, but it's deemed manageable or temporary, so we act on it.

Having said this, you might notice that some people are more comfortable with taking on risky, dangerous, or threatening situations. This stems from a number of reasons, which will be covered later in this chapter. However, it ultimately translates to having a stronger foundation, one that either has fewer veins of anxiety running through it (less weak spots due to more careful nurturing in early years, or perhaps genetic markers) or a greater familiarity with these veins and, therefore, a better understanding of how to soften, or calm, the impacts should they start to shake.

Let's take the scenario of crossing a road. How confident and familiar we are in any given situation will contribute to how safe we feel, and this will have an impact on our decision-making. A local Egyptian man will step out onto a busy six-lane road with not so much as a hint of anxiety, whereas a tourist will stand on the side of that road waiting for a larger gap that never seems to come.

We often make choices without realizing anxiety plays a role. Some will consistently leave the house early as they want to avoid being late. Perhaps this is due to having been late in the past and having a sense of guilt about it, or perhaps it's out of respect for others and not related to anxiety at all. Others might cling to their partner or control their movements because they have been abandoned or cheated on in the past. We study extra hard, perhaps because we were laughed at for not knowing an answer in class, out of fear of our parents' disapproval, or fear of being seen as a failure by others. We do these things often without knowing exactly why we do them. We are not always aware of the anxiety that drove the decision. These "milder" levels of anxiety drive our actions so as to avoid a "severe" level of anxiety.

Many of our choices are anxiety-driven, not necessarily due to high anxiety, but a level of anxiety. Milder anxiety is used to prevent significant anxiety (or panic). Often, when faced with these severe levels of anxiety or panic, we learn to take steps to avoid that in the future. This is a learned safety mechanism, and it underlies a great deal of our short- and long-term decision-making, often without realizing it, or put otherwise, it is often an unconscious decision-making process.

Keep it simple: Our minds are built on a metaphorical foundation that has veins of anxiety running through it. We did not build this foundation, nor the anxiety; rather, it was built for us, or more so, built into us by various forces. When anxiety strikes, it rattles our mental house, impairing our functioning until the anxiety is managed, dissipates, or resolves on its own. We often unconsciously engage in behaviors to prevent this shaking, typically by avoiding triggers rather than actively addressing them.

There are some people who always seem to have some level of anxiety in their life. However, this is not to say that people are destined to be unstable or in a state of anxiety forever. It is a matter of being aware of the anxiety and working towards reducing its impacts. Unfortunately, people often lean towards avoiding what causes anxiety rather than learning how to cope with and reduce its impact over time.

For example, those who fear public speaking tend not to take up jobs where speaking in front of others would ever be required. This may prevent them from becoming anxious, but it does nothing to remove that vein of anxiety from their foundation, and so that vein remains there, waiting to be triggered should they ever need to speak in front of a crowd, no matter how small or familiar that crowd may be. Having said that, should they successfully avoid this situation for their entire existence, then they will never trigger that anxiety. So perhaps it is an effective albeit limited and risky solution.

Should the person, however, be able to *remove* the vein of anxiety around public speaking, then there will be nothing in that foundation to cause anxiety. Whether they never have to speak in public or do so regularly, there will be no anxiety to be felt. This is what we would call targeting the root of the problem rather than simply avoiding the trigger for it. I would argue this to be a more functional and real solution. However, it requires effort and facing one's fears and anxiety. For that reason, people do not take this route often, opting to simply avoid triggers rather than remove causes.

So, what are these veins of anxiety that run through our foundation? How did they get there, and why do they shake the rest of the house, at times to the point of poor function or breakdown?

We have already touched on how anxiety is a fear response, which leads us to understand that something we are anxious about is something we fear. Also, we tend to fear things that are dangerous to us, things we do not understand, or things that can legitimately harm us. These could be physical, emotional, social, or financial things.

These veins of anxiety are all the things in your life that you fear: things you never learned to understand, things that you see as dangerous, things that are bigger or stronger than you are or can injure you. To be more specific, you may be anxious or fearful of snakes because you know they can injure or kill you. You may be anxious about talking to people because you had bad experiences or were never taught good social skills, which led to you fearing being socially injured in some way. You might fear attempting certain tasks because you fear the possibility of failure, which could lead to feeling like a failure—a significant emotional and potentially social setback. The reason you fear failure is probably due to a lack of encouragement and support in your early years. In fact, many anxieties will stem from a lack of support, encouragement, or guidance in our early years. We tend to learn physical safety via rough-and-tumble play and social interactions as children, but how do we learn emotional safety? We learn that from our parents. Did they comfort us and teach us how to manage emotions, how to understand them, and how they are temporary and will pass in time? Our parents (or general caregivers) teach us to cope with our emotions and provide a safe haven in our times of need. Should these physical and emotional safeties not be present in our childhood, we can understandably start to fear physical or emotional encounters.

If a child's need for shelter and protection from predators is not met by their parents, they may develop a hyper-vigilant manner and experience heightened anxiety about their safety and survival. Similarly, a child in need of love and support may develop a vein of anxiety about their lovability, impacting their ability to form intimate relationships in the future. They might avoid such relationships due to uncertainty about navigating them, or conversely, they might seek constant sources of love and affection to fill this void.

In essence, anxiety often develops due to a lack of development in childhood, but it can also develop later in life due to sufficiently impactful negative experiences. Overall, if we feel we are equipped to face what life and the world throws at us, we won't be anxious, at least not overwhelmingly so.

The Takeaway

The Anxiety Foundation is an attempt at representing how otherwise well-functioning individuals can be triggered by specific things in life that cause them to become overwhelmed by anxiety. It often traces back to something they needed for healthy development as a child but did not get. Other times, anxiety arises from an event or a series of events, which causes the person to question if they can "cope" or manage certain things. It creates doubt in their minds, so they start to fear the possible negative, damaging impact of the thing that is causing them anxiety. No matter how you look at it, anxiety shakes our foundations and everything built upon them. It stems from a fear of potential harm—whether physical, emotional, social, or financial.

Variation in Anxiety levels

Let's examine specific scenarios to understand why some people experience anxiety in certain situations while others do not. By doing this, we can also begin to identify potential *cures* or solutions for anxiety and how to overcome it.

It is important to remember the key points we've covered about anxiety, especially that it is triggered when we perceive a threat or danger.

This is crucial because if we do not perceive a situation as a threat, we will not experience an anxiety response. This highlights the fact that anxiety will not manifest unless we perceive a situation as threatening or are aware of its potential threat. This means that two people can be exposed to the same situation, and one perceives it as dangerous while the other does not. Why is this?

Scenario 1: A dark alley

The context for this scenario is a simple one:
Imagine having to walk down a dark alley late at night. Let's assume that in each scenario, Person 1 is anxious while Person 2 is not.

Controlling for physicality

Let's assume that Persons 1 and 2 are relatively similar individuals: 25-year-old males of similar stature. What might cause Person 1 to be anxious while Person 2 is not? The initial consideration (given that we have controlled for physicality) would be something to do with their thoughts or past experiences. Perhaps Person 1's anxiety comes from a previous negative experience in alleyways or perhaps a lack of familiarity with them, so he freezes, and the anxiety builds as he stares down that alley, trying to work out what to do. Meanwhile, Person 2 has walked hundreds of dark alleys with no negative experiences. Perhaps Person 2 is so fixated on getting home that he didn't even notice the dark alley before he was already through it.

Variable physicality

But what else could it be? Perhaps Person 1 is a 12-year-old girl of small stature, while Person 2 is a 30-year-old, six-foot-tall world champion cage fighter with a military background. So, it stands to reason that Person 1 might be anxious, while Person 2 might be less anxious. It's pretty understandable that the person who is well equipped to protect themselves is less frightened about what may happen in the alleyway.

But it is also possible that in this case, it's the 30-year-old who is frightened, while the 12-year-old is not. How? Well, perhaps the 30-year-old has a title fight next week and cannot risk a possible mugging, while the 12-year-old is simply oblivious to the danger and is only thinking about getting home on time.

As we can see, there are any number of possible contributing or mitigating factors when it comes to whether or not someone will become anxious in a given situation. In the examples above, we have seen that some of these factors include physicality, past experience, exposure or familiarity, one's awareness or focus on the dangers, as well as one's future focus and considering if the risk is a timely one.

After using just one setting (the alleyway), two scenarios (physically matched and physically unmatched), and only a brief review of them, we have come up with at least five possible reasons for differing levels of anxiety between two people. Alongside that, we found that in the second test case, although we can take a reasonable guess as to who will feel the anxiety, we cannot derive this with absolute certainty. Furthermore, this assumes that the alley is dangerous at all. In truth, there are any number of other possible factors to consider in these scenarios, from personality to habits, conditioning, etc. What is important here is that there can be a lot of factors behind what contributes to an anxiety response, whilst other times, it's a very straightforward trigger.

At this point, it may seem like we have only moved further away from, or complicated, identifying what we need to do to prevent or reduce the likelihood that someone will become anxious. But I would argue that there is a much simpler solution. You may have noticed that we've started focusing on the complexities involved in solving anxiety—there are numerous factors that can contribute to the issue. However, if we take a step back from this and simplify matters, the answer can become clearer. Perhaps that answer is clear to you already.

What is the common thread in the above scenario? Across both test cases and all factors that we did identify, even if you consider possible biological reasons for becoming anxious, what is it that determines who, if anyone, becomes anxious? I'd encourage you to stop and consider this and see if you can find it for yourself before reading on. If you believe you have an answer, note it down and then think of more, not because there are many answers, but because finding the right one on your own will serve you better than reading on and being told. Take a minute or a month if you need to or go back over the above scenario until you find it. If you are not sure about your answer, read Scenario 2 and see if that clarifies things in your mind. Or, if you just want some answers, read on.

Scenario 2: A dark alley with two scowling men intent to attack

We take the same dark alley from Scenario 1, but this time, we add two visible adult males standing mid-way down that alley.

Controlling for physicality

We take the same two 25-year-old males of similar stature. Person 1 takes one look at that alleyway and is instantly anxious, so much so that they cannot bring themselves to walk down it and decide to take a different route home. Person 2 also sees the two men, but after the initial pang of anxiety, he takes a strong and confident posture and walks down the alleyway. He has decided that although there is a potential threat, he is not convinced that it is one that will eventuate. He takes his chances and passes through. He does not *perceive* the threat as large or likely enough to warrant him altering his path home. Perhaps he is very familiar with the pathway, perhaps he has walked past these men before, or perhaps he feels he could avoid them if needed.

Variable physicality

The 12-year-old girl and the 30-year-old cage fighter face the dark alley with two loitering men. The initial expectation here would be that the 12-year-old girl will have a great deal of anxiety. However, this may not always be true. Had this girl only ever been exposed to kindness from strangers or never been taught the potential dangers of strangers, then she may have absolutely no understanding of the danger. She does not *perceive* a threat, and so her anxiety or fear is not triggered. In fact, she may be more anxious about an empty dark alley as there could be "monsters." Whereas if there are two men in the alley, and men have always been nice and protective towards her, then by her reckoning, she may well feel safer in this scenario than in the first.

The 30-year-old cage fighter has a similar range of variability around whether or not he is anxious. On the one hand, he knows he is a championship-level fighter, so it's likely these two random men spending time in an alley may not pose much of a threat at all. Then again, as a grown man, he has the presence of mind to consider that they may have weapons, they may be desperate, or there may be more of them just out of his line of sight. The more he thinks about it, the more likely he is to identify *possible* threats that he cannot yet see, and this may cause him to *not* walk down that alley. If he doesn't think too far ahead, he may well back himself and take that alley home.

The Counter to Anxiety

Spoiler alert for those aiming to solve it themselves: this next section provides the answer.

In the above cases, regardless of their size, past experience, beliefs, points of focus, etc., they are all going through the same scenario: the same alley with the same level of danger. Even if there is some biological marker that makes them more likely to become anxious or if they have been conditioned to be scared of their own shadow, what ultimately determines their anxiety levels and, therefore, their decision/ability to walk down that alleyway is their *confidence* in their ability to do so successfully.

In our first scenario, there is no overt threat present. It is simply a dark alleyway. There is no immediate danger in that alleyway, only the *potential* of an unseen danger that one creates in one's mind. Largely, this scenario spawns anxiety via a person's inner thoughts or inner dialogue. This is what will determine whether they *feel* safe. If their thoughts, or self-talk, are one of safety, then they will not *feel* anxious, as they will *believe* they are relatively safe. This, however, does not mean that it is a safe scenario; it simply means they believe it to be safe enough. Equally, the reverse is true. One's thoughts may convince them the alley is dangerous, so they *feel* anxiety due to thinking it is unsafe. However, it may well be just an alleyway with no present dangers. The reality of how safe or dangerous the alley is will not be known for certain until one walks it, but our mind will sculpt a view of it for itself and it does this based on what it has been taught up until that point, specifically, what it has been taught about dark alleyways and what it believes about one's own abilities. If people believe in themselves and their abilities, then they have the confidence to walk that alleyway, either without anxiety or with a healthy level of it.

Things do change in Scenario 2, at least to some extent. With a real and present danger, the manifestation of anxiety is no longer just one in your mind, so we cannot simply say that the anxiety is all internally generated. We could logically assume that there would be more anxiety in Scenario 2 than in Scenario 1. The 12-year-old girl is very likely to be anxious unless she is completely oblivious to the danger before her or has somehow been led to believe she could outmaneuver the men and make it across safely. The two 25-year-old males are highly likely to feel anxiety and would likely only walk that dark alleyway if they had an over-inflated sense of self or an unhelpfully large ego. Only the 30-year-old ex-military world champion fighter realistically feels that the threat may not be great enough to make him re-route or avoid the alleyway.

So again, this comes down to one's *confidence* in their ability to navigate the threat ahead of them or their ability to even identify the threat in the first instance. So perhaps confidence combined with the accuracy of one's threat perception is key to managing one's anxiety and, indeed, safety.

In reality, there may be some freak possibility that the 12-year-old girl makes it through that alleyway; perhaps she is very nimble and quick, perhaps one of the assailants slips, and the other has a bout of guilt. It is also possible that the ex-military 30-year-old does not overpower the assailants. Ultimately, one's anxiety does not come from an outcome but from one's belief in their ability to tackle the problem.

The young girl may overcome her anxiety, try the alleyway, and succeed or fail. However, whether or not she becomes anxious is dependent on her assessment of her safety in that alleyway. Either she feels safe due to not perceiving the threat or due to feeling she can outrun them; either way, her belief in being safe or not will determine her anxiety levels. The same process occurs in the ex-military cage fighter. His anxiety levels stem from his confidence in his ability, both physically to defend himself and mentally to analyze the threat effectively. He may succeed or he may not, but his level of anxiety was based on his "belief" in himself to succeed.

What do we learn from this? How can we use this to help ourselves?

Keep it simple: Anxiety does not come from an outcome but from one's belief in one's ability to remain safe or to succeed in a situation. It stems from how confident one is in tackling a situation.

Confidence can be global or specific. However, in terms of anxiety, we cannot be both confident and anxious about the same thing at the same time. One will outweigh the other, and whichever is greater will govern your action. For example, one may be confident in getting through Scenario 2 but not confident in cooking a five-course meal for seven, or dancing a tango without tearing a ligament. Confidence levels are subject to the task at hand. This battle between confidence and anxiety plays out in any given scenario. If people can build their confidence in all scenarios, they will resolve their anxiety. More accurately, they will resolve any *problematic* anxiety. We should always keep in mind that anxiety is a very useful and helpful mechanism. It is that same anxiety that will prevent you from putting yourself in very real danger.

One caveat here is that of possible strong biological influences. It may well be the case that a person has some significant neurological difference, which plays an overwhelming part in their ability to manage anxiety. Equally, someone with significant trauma may also have a hyper-aroused nervous system, which may greatly impact their ability to regulate themselves.

Keep it simple: Anxiety stems from our perceiving something as a threat. We are more likely to see threats in things we do not understand, are not comfortable with, or do not believe we can overcome. The greater our skill sets and belief in these skill sets, the less likely we are to feel anxiety or at least feel overcome by that anxiety. Create ability and confidence, and you remove anxiety. That is, of course, assuming there is no underlying and overwhelming biological contributor.

The Confidence Analogy

Confidence is something that is built over time, and although the principle of how to do this is the same across all cases, there are some complicating factors. This can generally be broken down into two categories, which I'll refer to as "building confidence" and "repairing confidence."

In my clinical practice, I have found that when trying to explain psychological concepts such as confidence, it is often made easier via the use of analogies rather than a clinical textbook approach. After all, clients did not come for a lecture but for *personalized* help. So, in this case, let's make the analogy between confidence and physical strength.

At the risk of oversimplifying and enraging every personal trainer out there, physical strength is generally built by repeatedly lifting heavy things! If we do this consistently, we will gradually become stronger. The same applies to confidence. If you successfully achieve things over and over, you will grow your confidence in that thing. Let's see if we can develop this understanding of confidence overcoming anxiety by playing out this analogy some more.

CHAPTER 1 – ANXIETY

Those of you who are more fitness-informed will know that if you lift something too heavy, you will fail at that lift and may even injure yourself in the process. This also holds true with confidence. If you take on a task that you are bound to fail, you will lose confidence. You may even think you can never achieve that task and forever lack confidence in yourself in that department. Going back to our fitness gurus, they will also no doubt tell you that if you work your way up slowly, you stand a great chance of getting that heavy lift eventually. Again, the same holds for confidence: set smaller, more achievable goals, and watch your confidence grow over time to a point where you believe you can do something you never thought possible!

I can hear some of you thinking, "Yes, but strength depends on more than just consistency of lifting! It also depends on many other things such as genetics, diet, technique, and strength of supporting ligaments." I also hear the personal trainers saying, "...and how good your trainer is!"

Granted, all of these, and likely more factors, will play a role in how successful you are in lifting something heavy. So, let's see how long this analogy between strength and confidence goes. Let's take a look at how each of the factors above might be represented in the case of confidence and, therefore, anxiety. Table 1 shows the parallels of this analogy, followed by some justification below.

Table 1: The strength/confidence analogy

Strength	Confidence
Genetics	Genetics
Diet	Childhood learning and Experiences
Technique	Skills, Knowledge, Thoughts
Supporting ligaments	Supportive People/Community
Coach/Personal Trainer	Yourself, Partner, Friends, Mentor, Therapist

Genetics

I'm no geneticist, but as most of us understand, our genetics create certain features and limitations to who we are on a cellular level. I do not question that there are some who have a more active anxiety response than others; some even have an underdeveloped amygdala, which can reduce the intensity of your response to threats. Neuroplasticity may compensate for some of these things; however, how the brain may compensate for such things is beyond the scope of this book. Suffice it to say that there may be some genetic factors that we cannot overcome. However, how can we know the true limits of our genetics without constantly pushing against them? At times, we can be too hasty in blaming genetics rather than blaming our levels of effort, especially effort, when it comes to facing and overcoming discomfort.

Diet/Childhood Experience

Just as one's diet provides good or bad fuel for the body's ability to perform, our childhood experiences provide good or bad fuel for the mind in tackling the world. This childhood develops a sense of self and self-belief. A child who is raised with love, encouragement, and support could be seen as having a good emotional diet that builds their self-esteem, confidence, and belief in themselves. In comparison, a child raised in constant negativity, abuse, neglect, and relentless insults towards their ability will develop only self-doubt, negativity, fear, and no sense of confidence in their ability. Our emotional well-being plays a very strong role in what actions we do and do not undertake and, therefore, what we do and do not learn to do.

Technique/Skills, Knowledge, Thoughts

As any sports coach out there will attest to, the proper technique does not just help you to lift heavier heavy things but also helps you lift heavy things with less effort, all while reducing the risk of injury and failure. Raw strength is not everything. If you learn the right technique, you can rely less on your physical strength. Equally, if you learn the right mental techniques, you can rely less on raw willpower or self-belief. You can learn to talk yourself through the process and rely on your thoughts and knowledge to help you through something difficult. For example, the knowledge that all emotions are temporary and that they are bound to pass can help provide you with a little more peace of mind to get you through a difficult situation. Likewise, knowing how to read other people's body language or what language to use in certain situations can help you to be more socially confident and overcome social anxiety.

Supporting Ligaments/Supportive People/Community

Our bodies are a complex weave of muscles, ligaments, tendons, bones, and all manner of other things. Muscles may do the bulk of the work, but if they are not securely pinned down to a bone, or if that bone is broken, then the muscle will not be able to do its job. This is much the same with anxiety, confidence, and mental health in general. A person may be strong, confident, and capable, but they get that way in part due to those around them. They can be confident because they know they are loved, and they have been assisted along the way by others. The muscle/confidence is only as big as it is because of the support structures around it. We are well aware of "the home ground advantage" in sports, where the team or individual performs better when cheered on by their local support team. We know that people generally run faster and lift heavier when others are present than when alone. So, too, is the case with issues of mental health, including anxiety and confidence. You need only look at any child playing sports and how happy and confident they are when they have their supportive parents watching on, cheering on, and yelling supportive messages. Or perhaps the opposite, a child who feels fear and panic at the sight of their abusive parent in the stands demanding they do better, or they will be punished when they return home. Our levels of confidence are often built up by the messages of others, particularly important others in our lives, such as parents, friends, and partners.

Trainer/You, Friends, Therapist, Elder

Personal trainers, as I understand it, are the ones who stand alongside you, guide you, push you, and help you improve your goals. They do this with their underlying knowledge of the body and of various training techniques to get the most out of the body, as well as likely having a friendly and supportive manner. They are informed, trusted, and supportive of your needs while firm in pushing you to improve. This is much like a trusted friend, a wise elder, a therapist, and also yourself.

The personal trainer is both a voice and a figure that we put trust in to help us with our goals, just as a therapist might be with mental health or general mental development. It could also be an elder, a trusted family member, or a friend. In any case, it is an external voice and source of confidence. We are not sure if we can achieve a particular lift or task, so we look to the trainer or therapist for the support and confidence to make an attempt. Hopefully, over time, that voice and belief of the trainer or therapist/elder starts to be taken on board, and the voice and confidence start to be your own. The external support becomes internal support; their voice and belief in you become your voice and belief in yourself. And so, you become the source of confidence over time. In other words, our *self-talk* perpetuates our confidence over time.

Keep it simple: Confidence and our beliefs are a large part of overcoming anxiety. It is built in us over time, with what we hear in childhood playing a big role. Whether we realize it or not, others have impacted our levels of confidence, and over time, we either choose to develop it or allow it to be controlled by others. Genetics may also play a role; however, with the right support and efforts, we can all improve our levels of confidence and reduce our levels of anxiety.

So, we know that confidence is a belief in ourselves that we can overcome or achieve something. If we have sufficient belief in ourselves, then we make the attempt. Should we fail at something, our confidence can, and often does, take a knock. If we have enough confidence in hand, then this knock does little if any damage, and we try again. If, however, we have very little confidence to spare, that knock could be enough for us to quit. Your levels of confidence begin to form based on the messages you received as a child. As you grow older, your confidence is further influenced by your successes or failures and the messages you and others associate with these outcomes. One can also work at one's confidence levels by learning new things and gathering skills and knowledge, which they put into practice. Over time, these skills improve, and you grow in your belief in your capabilities and become more confident. Of course, should your environment be filled with voices that minimize, deny, or fail to acknowledge your achievements, your confidence could start to decline.

Keep it simple: Confidence initially comes from what you were told as a child. Encouragement and support will breed confidence, while criticism and neglect will erode it. As we age, our confidence is impacted by the voices or judgments of those around us, as well as our own voice and judgment toward ourselves. Effort towards skills development via practice will, over time, increase confidence, assuming it is accompanied by a positive, supportive voice.

How does one obtain confidence? Through our parents as children, through the judgments and supports of our peers as adolescents, and through other important people as adults. Additionally, and most importantly, our confidence is very highly impacted by our own voice. How we speak to ourselves and what we convince ourselves of will have one of the biggest impacts on our confidence. As children, our self-talk is greatly influenced by our parents' voices. We tend to mimic them in everything we do, including the words they use towards us. This shifts to our friends during adolescence and then our partners in adulthood.

In short, we obtain confidence from the opinions of others. Only later in life, and only if one makes an effort, can we obtain confidence from ourselves. If you put in the effort to improve at any given task or skill and accompany this with an accurate and supportive voice/thought/dialogue with yourself, then you can very much gain confidence and, as a result, reduce anxiety.

Elements of Anxiety
Pervasiveness

Confidence is difficult to build while anxiety exists. To make things worse, anxiety often finds ways to ingrain itself, like tendrils weaving throughout your mind, getting in deep, and seating itself behind every neuron it can find. It lays seeds anywhere and everywhere and is desperate to crop up at any opportunity. It often takes the form of doubt, reminding you that you are not good enough, that you will fail, and that you cannot do any better. Many with anxiety will know these statements all too well, as will anyone with a narcissistic or sociopathic partner!

Anxiety doesn't care for truth; it has a very strong and unbending narrative of its own, and it won't let the truth or reality get in the way of complete dominance of your mind and body. It will repeat itself as often as it can, finding any real-life scenario to prove that you are inadequate, or it will invent one in your imagination to make you believe things that never actually happened.

Anxiety can be relentless; it will take any opportunity to try and repeat its negative commentary. It will often be at its loudest when you are at your quietest or when you are facing something it has convinced you is dangerous. It can be merciless as it attacks you with its negativity when all you are trying to do is sleep after a long and exhausting day. It has no issue in attacking you when you are at your weakest. It will convince you of things that never happened and deny you of the good things that did. It does all the things that a kind, caring, loving, supportive voice would *not* do.

Anxiety convinces you that it is *you!* It convinces you that *you* are saying these things to yourself, that you think them, and therefore, they must be true because we all believe that what we think is right. If it convinces you that it *is* you, then it essentially owns you. But anxiety, or anxious thinking, is just that—a thought in your mind. It is *not* your actual mind; you are not anxiety. Anxiety is merely a thought you have. Of course, anxiety won't tell you this. It won't tell you that it is just a weed in your mind that you can choose to ignore or even replace with a thought of your own choosing or creation! No, it banks on the idea that if you never challenge it, then anxiety will have its way and get to live on. The fact that this means your life suffers is of no concern to anxiety itself; it's a parasite.

As soon as one realizes that they are not their anxiety, they can start to choose to remove this weed. They can realize that the anxious thoughts are not so much their thoughts but rather an echo of someone else's voice or an echo in an empty cavern that should have been filled with kindness, support, education, or acceptance but somehow wasn't.

The Advertising Campaign

We have known for some time now that the more you repeat a message, the more likely you are to remember it. This also holds true for believing it! Tell any child something enough times, and they will simply accept it as true, regardless of how absurd it is. It does not take long to see this in action.

Children tend to believe in things like Santa Claus and the Tooth Fairy and that babies grow in a cabbage patch or are delivered by a stork. Tell them something, and they tend to believe it. Adults are often not much better. Have you ever wondered why massive companies still spend billions of dollars on advertising every year? It's because they know that if they continue to transmit their message to your brain, then you are likely to believe it. If they tell you enough times that acid water tastes good, you will eventually believe it. And if that sounds crazy, just ask yourself if you have ever enjoyed soda.

There are any number of products that are objectively bad for your health, yet people consume them without pause. Why? Not because they are of benefit to them but because they have heard the message so many times that they believe it. They have had that advertising campaign in their eyes and ears repeatedly, often without noticing. So, after a time, they simply come to believe what is being said. Anxiety works in the same way. It launches an advertising campaign in your mind. It does so under the guise of safety while neglecting to point out how damaging it is to you. Drinking soda makes you feel good at the expense of being good for you, just as anxiety makes you feel good/safe (by avoiding something you fear) at the expense of being good for you. At least those company advertising campaigns are only for a few minutes at a time and can be turned off or challenged by others, whereas anxiety happens 24 hours a day, is hard to turn off, and no one can see or hear it to help you challenge it!

Weeds and Flowers (Anxiety and Confidence)

The lucky ones had parents that made sure this weed never took hold. They filled that child with praise, encouragement, validation, and compassionate correction and made sure to treat them with respect. Those kids did what all kids do; they started to copy their parents and treated themselves with the kindness and respect their parents showed. Whether they know it or not, the parents were putting down good fertilizer for the mind and helping to prevent a future weed infestation. But not all of us were so lucky.

Some of us did not have those compassionate, loving parents or did not have them for long enough. Others fell in with peers who undid the good work of parents and muddied the waters enough to give weeds a foothold. Sadly, some of us had parents who spread nothing but violence, negativity, insults, and all manner of abuse or neglect, leaving nothing but weeds in their children's minds. For some, weeds are all they know, and flowers are so foreign that should one happen to sprout, they pull them up by the root and throw them away. They are so uncomfortable with anything other than weeds that they simply cannot accept anything nice or nurturing in their own worlds.

The Propagation

Keeping in mind our different starting points in terms of anxiety and confidence, let's consider what maintains that garden of weeds (anxiety) and flowers (confidence). The mechanism here is not much different. All that changes is that the advertising campaign changes hands from the parents to the individual. The individual now propagates the negative messaging and the fear and doubt campaign. In the case of someone with confidence, the positive, supportive, kind thinking towards themselves continues. These are the lucky ones, the ones with self-respect who will not put up with being treated poorly for long; they know not to let such weeds into their mind garden. Unfortunately, those who are less lucky either do not know how to defend against letting weeds in or are simply so desperate to have anything in their mind garden they will accept whatever comes along.

A Solution

If you have gotten this far, a solution may already be apparent to you. Rip up the weeds and plant the flowers, right? Well, in some cases, yes, this is a natural epiphany, and people can shift their lives drastically. But if it was so easy, we would have eradicated anxiety some time ago.

In truth, this can be a very difficult task, a task that gets increasingly difficult the more convinced a person is that their advertising campaign is the truth. After all, the longer you have heard something, the more likely you are to *believe* it, and by believe, I do mean that it becomes a *belief* the person holds. Much as a staunch religious believer is unlikely to simply stop believing because they are told they are wrong, so too, someone with anxiety is unlikely to simply stop being anxious by being told their beliefs are wrong. In both situations, if you tell these people they are wrong, they will likely shut you out and dismiss anything else you may have to say on the matter. To them, you become less credible than a total stranger who agrees with their beliefs and reinforces them. These individuals prefer someone who validates their beliefs rather than challenges them.

Remember, anxiety/weeds do not allow the truth to get in their way. They have no interest in truth, only in continuing to exist. Anxiety has spent a lot of time and effort convincing the person that it is a part of them or that it *is* them. Sadly, some people with anxiety lack a solid foundation for understanding their own worth. Their parents, consumed by jealousy or insecurity, fail to affirm their child's intelligence, humor, or creativity. Instead of nurturing their child, these parents project their own issues onto them and never acknowledging the child's true identity. What chance does such a child have to develop confidence or even a remotely accurate self-identity? In such a child's world, the only reality they know is that negative advertising campaign.

So where does this leave those who cannot simply rip out the weeds and accept that they are not what the anxiety tells them they are? Start slow. Try having them pick out just one weed or a leaf from that weed. Or, in real terms, have them question one of these thoughts and ask themselves how accurate that thought/belief is. Let me be clear: let "them" question it and avoid doing this for them if you can. Provide them with a question or an idea, but let them do the questioning; otherwise, you run the risk of being the person they believe is lying to them. Perhaps this is you simply handing them a spade so they can decide how to use it and when. Over time, you can start handing them some flower seeds and help them water them by telling them what *you* see in them. Your role in helping them question their anxiety is akin to aiding them in the process of uprooting those negative thoughts. When they begin to question these thoughts themselves, it's like they are actively pulling out the weeds of doubt and insecurity within their own minds. Over time, as these weeds of anxiety weaken, the soil metaphorically becomes fertile ground where seeds of compliments and positive reinforcement can be planted. By showing and telling them what you see in them, you help them recognize their own strengths and capabilities. Engaging in activities together further nurtures their belief in their potential to learn and grow. This supportive and compassionate presence acts like a stake supporting a young plant, helping them gain enough strength and confidence to eventually flourish independently.

CHAPTER 1 – ANXIETY

This solution is by no means groundbreaking, but neither is the idea of watering a plant to keep it alive. Anyone can do it, as long as they know how much to water and how often. My intent here is not to manufacture some new and mind-blowing approach to deal with anxiety. Many have solved this problem well before I came to understand it. The objective here is to provide a simple but effective understanding of what anxiety is, how it comes about, and how it stays alive.

The analogy of weeds and plants is easily interchangeable with anything that requires growth. In fact, the more you look at dynamics within humans, the more you see similarities in the world. The macro and the micro seem to reflect each other everywhere. Mental health, sport, physical health, relationships, academics, art, music, and nature all share similarities in their development and positive and negative influences and can largely all be viewed and improved on in similar terms.

By helping someone develop confidence or build their "self-esteem," you are helping them fight their anxiety. After all, if they feel they are a strong, capable person who can ensure their own survival, then they have little reason to feel anxious or at least little reason to have problematic anxiety. The same principle holds true for those trying to help themselves out of their anxiety issues. At the core, they need to start to develop their sense of safety or confidence in their ability to ensure their own safety. Of course, while not impossible, it is much more difficult for an adult to do this for themselves. In truth, it is easier to instill confidence in another than it is for yourself.

The Role of Achievement

As a core tenant, the more you do or achieve, the more confident you become in yourself. Even if you only ever do that thing at an average level compared to others, you are now at least confident of your ability or skill and can predict your likely outcome. You do not need to have a perfect outcome for a task; you only need to know what the likely outcome is. The more certainty you have, the less anxiety, in theory, you'll experience.

Knowing your capability across many tasks gives you a better sense of who you are. Importantly, however, we must practice these tasks and not simply believe that if we did poorly at something once or twice, that means we are poor at the task. We can only truly know the limits of our ability by constantly pushing against those limits. Every elite athlete is only at the top of their discipline due to constantly pushing against what their limit was previously. Only by doing this do they determine what they are truly capable of. The same goes for any human trait, be it creativity, empathy, anxiety, confidence, etc.

It is often our belief in ourselves that limits our outcomes, even if these beliefs are not rooted in reality. A narcissist can have ultimate belief in themselves, and they have no end of confidence. They may have objectively poor skills at a given task, but because they refuse to believe it, they remain confident as they *believe* they are still the greatest! This tends to keep them doggedly persisting at something, which often results in improvements. We see the opposite cycle in those with anxiety and low self-esteem.

Keep it simple: The better you know your capability at any given task, the more certainty you have and, therefore, the less anxiety you are likely to experience.

All of this is why we should make an effort to *try* or practice things so we're able to know our abilities and limits. The more certain we are of our ability, regardless of how high or low that ability is, then the more certain we are of the likely outcome. If you know you are not a natural athlete, then you won't expect to win or even do well at a running event. In fact, you can expect to finish at the tail end of the field and not have this be a point of negative reflection. You will also likely know that your skill sets rest in other areas, and that becomes what you identify with or draw general confidence from. Develop realistic expectations of yourself based on what you have learned about your abilities as an individual.

Keep it simple: Anxiety reduces as confidence increases, and your confidence can be built by acknowledging your successes and not amplifying your failings. Understanding your abilities and limitations will increase your confidence in achieving outcomes, which can reduce anxiety.

Building Confidence

Here are some straightforward, practical tips to help you move from feeling anxious to becoming confident:

- Be aware of your anxiety and develop your understanding of why it exists.
- Put aside what your inner dialogue/monologue is telling you about your ability. Ignore it, challenge it, and start to change its language, but do not accept it as truth.
- Start setting goals, go out and achieve something. Start small and make it reasonable and measurable. Perhaps you want to improve your running or walk more, or you want to learn to cook. Whatever it is, set that task, then do it again and again and again, and do not stop until you are satisfied with your result. You may win, lose, or draw, none of which are relevant. All that matters is you improve to a level you are satisfied with, or at the very least, learn your limit in that skill.
- Importantly, whatever the outcomes of your attempts, always view the outcome objectively and always give yourself credit for any gain or accomplishment.
- Never allow your self-talk to be unduly harsh or unkind. Only ever speak to yourself as you would to your beloved child: build yourself up, credit yourself when you are successful, and encourage yourself when you are not. At the very least, accept your limitations and realize they are important.

Note: Anxiety, much like confidence, exhibits certain quirks: Neither is universal, both can vary over short or extended periods, and neither requires accuracy to manifest—belief alone is sufficient.

Understanding Our Environments

One of the side effects of the brain having this specter of anxiety underlying its foundation is the desire to be aware of the world it lives in. The desire to be aware of your environment. On a basic level, this means the physical environment; your brain wants to know if the physical setting is safe or if it's standing on a cliff edge. The more accurate our understanding of the environment is, the better placed we are to maintain our safety or survival. Going one step further than understanding the environment is controlling it. If we can manipulate our environment enough to be in control of it, our safety and survival are even more assured. For now, let's look at this "understanding" of the environment.

As adults, our environments expand from the physical to the social, cultural, professional, intellectual, and so on. As adults, we find that these environments tend to dominate our day-to-day lives. The physical environment is already largely understood and secured, but these other, less tangible environments are far more complex, more changing, and typically of far greater importance to our survival.

To complicate matters, we often cannot trust any of our five senses to accurately navigate these adult environments. How a person looks may not be representative of how they are as a person, and what they say may or may not be honest or accurate. What tastes good may not be good for you, etc. The very senses that served us well as a child and taught us how to survive the world are no longer so reliable.

So, how do we navigate this complex, intangible, adult world full of invisible threats? Luckily, by our mid-20s, we are armed with a fully grown adult brain. To us, it is as invisible as those complex social, financial, and emotional threats, so we use the invisible to navigate the invisible, and we think our way through. We use our thoughts,

CHAPTER 1 – ANXIETY

beliefs, assumptions, or guesses to try and put together a picture of our environment as accurately as we can. We improve with experience and get better at understanding these environments, and we start to rely on our thoughts to help us survive. We learn from others and ourselves what a good choice is and what a bad choice is. Perhaps we research what is healthy for our bodies. We start to make judgments about who is trustworthy and who is not. We will often ask others what they know or think about a given challenge in life, and we weigh this up against what others say and what we already think. But how reliable is all of this? How do we know who to believe or if what we already believe is right? As children, we touch a stone, and we know with certainty what it is, but as adults, we often have less certainty about what we think. Thoughts can change; we could be proven wrong or right, or we may simply adopt a different "belief" system. All this variability can become the perfect breeding ground for anxiety. After all, uncertainty is the path to anxiety, and these adult worlds have no shortage of uncertainty.

As social creatures, we often seek perspectives from others to validate our understanding of situations. When facing new environments or topics, relying solely on our own thoughts leaves room for uncertainty. Anxiety compels us to seek confirmation, preferably from experienced individuals like trusted parents or senior colleagues, who we believe have our best interests in mind. In healthy family dynamics, we trust our parents' guidance, even when we disagree (whereas in unhealthy, abusive, or neglectful families, we are either left without guidance, or lead to believe falsehoods about ourselves and the world). In workplaces, we often run things by senior colleagues for a reality check, assuming their experience offers a more accurate perspective. This process tests and refines our own understanding by comparing it with others' and ultimately boosting our confidence in navigating our surroundings.

The more of these "reality checks" that come back confirming what we already thought, the more confident we become in our brains' ability to understand its environment, and therefore, the more relaxed and confident we are in that environment.

The more capable and trustworthy people we have to do these reality checks with, the greater our chance of learning how to understand our environments. Armed with their helpful guidance, we learn to hone and trust our own thoughts and how to use them to navigate our adult environments.

With this trust in our abilities, we become confident and secure. Anxiety will be well managed as we trust ourselves to be able to navigate what comes next. However, if we lack these trusted and experienced people, this process may take longer, or we may never get to the stage of confidently understanding the environment at all. Over time, they may overcome this; however, we will be at a disadvantage to those who have never had to face such personal doubt. In the more extreme case where a person is surrounded by genuinely harmful or incompetent others, they are far more likely to never develop a strong sense of confidence in their ability to navigate an environment. They are at risk of developing debilitating levels of anxiety and panic and face very real struggles when having to navigate any complex adult environment. These are the cases where we often see things such as agoraphobia, social anxiety, panic disorder, as well as a host of trauma-based issues.

But what if these reality checks come back contrary to our thoughts? In these circumstances, several things can happen depending on the person's stage of development. It's possible that they take the conflicting information on board and "see what happens," learning from the outcome and seeing who was more accurate. They may simply not believe the reality check and stick with what they thought, or they might defer to the reality check and go against their own initial thought. In any case, when a reality check comes back counter to what we initially thought, there will always be a small sway in that anxiety foundation. This is perhaps why we tend not to like people who think differently from us or why it is hard to hear something that is not in line with what we already think. It causes us to question our thoughts or beliefs, which causes a ripple in our anxiety foundation, something very few of us enjoy.

CHAPTER 1 – ANXIETY

Generally speaking, the more one knows about a topic, the better one understands it, and hence, the more we reality check, the more we tend to understand our environments. Equally, the person who can tolerate ripples in their anxiety foundation is more likely to develop a broader, stronger, and more tolerant foundation. Through constant ripples, they learn they can trust their house to stay standing and hence do not fear the contrary opinions of others. In fact, they grow to value it.

Keep it simple: We seek reality checks from others to help us navigate our complex social worlds. The more aligned this feedback is to our own understanding, the more confident we become in ourselves, and the less anxiety we are likely to feel.

The Four Common Factors

With anxiety and confidence now covered, we can move on to the four common factors that I often see in the therapy room and out in the world. Each of these factors tend to apply to a particular part of a person's life. That is to say that those lacking an understanding of this factor tend to suffer in a particular realm of their life. For example, those who fail to take responsibility for themselves tend to have problems with their own personal development and in their relationships with others. Anxiety can play a big role in these factors and should always be considered as an underlying influence, hence why we've covered it in detail in this chapter.

As a reminder, the four factors, along with their areas of impact, are:
1. The Blame-Responsibility Dynamic (Personal Development and Relationships)
2. The Primary Pitfall (Awareness and Interpersonal Understanding)
3. Knowing the Cost (Decision Making)
4. The Take-home Message (Learning Bias and Attitude Development)

Chapter 2 – Factor 1: Introducing Blame and Responsibility

The Blame-Responsibility Dynamic often plays out in two circumstances: when there is a degree of conflict between two or more people and in a person's own development. The basic premise for this dynamic is simple: when there is conflict, there is often a struggle between blame and responsibility. That is to say, when something goes wrong, either blame or responsibility will be attributed somewhere by someone. How this plays out will determine how much of a conflict there is. This chapter will look at what role blame and responsibility play in conflicts and how to use them for your personal growth. The following chapters will look at the finer points of these dynamics, particularly how this dynamic can play out interpersonally and, to a degree, why we follow certain patterns within this dynamic.

As a caveat, I should state that a degree of other factors likely play a part in this dynamic, including things such as personality and attachment style, as well as developmental theories, such as those explored by Erikson and Piaget. However, for the purposes of getting the message across around this dynamic, we won't be addressing or overlapping these theories here. The first factor of the Blame-Responsibility Dynamic is strongly influenced by anxiety and confidence levels, so understanding those factors is vital.

Throughout my clinical work, this dynamic has become prominent over time. I do not believe this is due to it being a new phenomenon, but rather, it is easier to identify once the concept is well understood. Knowledge of the Blame-Responsibility Dynamic and understanding its roots provides a fundamental framework for identifying interpersonal conflicts. It has also become apparent how little insight many people have into this dynamic, or at least the damage it is causing them and their relationships.

Keep it simple: Whenever there is conflict or disharmony between two or more people, first look to see where the blame or responsibility is.

The Role of Responsibility in Conflict

It doesn't take much to realize that blame holds negative connotations. While some people tolerate it better than others, no one enjoys being blamed for things, especially when they are not at fault. Even when they are objectively to blame, it is still something people tend to avoid if they can. A classic example of this is the person sitting in a classroom quietly praying that the teacher does not blame them for talking in class when the guilty party is the person next to them. Being blamed for something, especially when we are innocent, will rouse a negative feeling in most, if not all, of us. Blame feels bad, and we tend to dislike and avoid it. We inherently associate negativity with blame; after all, when has anyone been "blamed" for scoring well on an exam or for showing someone kindness?

Responsibility, on the other hand, can hold either a negative or a positive connotation depending on the outcome. Some of us fear responsibility, while others take pride in it. Which direction this takes will depend on one's history with it, along with their levels of confidence and anxiety. Typically, when the outcome of taking responsibility is a good one, we will associate positivity with responsibility. However, should the outcome be negative or a failure, then taking responsibility suddenly isn't so desirable; it starts to "feel" as desirable as blame, and we can develop a negative connotation around it.

If we consider the idea that people want to feel good and want to feel good about themselves, then it is easy to see why we would want to avoid blame. Blame will inevitably bring negativity. Responsibility, on the other hand, is a mixed bag. So, this leaves us wanting to avoid blame and potentially avoid responsibility.

Our brain tends to want to understand its environment and what is happening in it. When there is an issue, such as something going wrong in general, then our brains want to understand what happened and what was responsible for it happening. Once our brain makes sense of what has happened, it will calm down, and our *Anxiety Foundation* will stop shaking, reassured that the world makes sense again. Therefore, we try to figure out who did what, which leads to assigning either responsibility or blame. If the guilty party takes responsibility, then our brain will feel relief; it has the reality check it needs to understand the environment, and we can move forward. However, if the guilty party does not take responsibility (because they fear it), then our brain feels no relief, there is no confirmation of reality, we now start to wonder who is responsible, and perhaps fear we will be "blamed." In fact, if the guilty party is avoiding responsibility, then it is quite likely that they *will* blame someone, and so your developing anxiety is warranted. This is our first peek at how this dynamic works and what drives it.

Keep it simple: Blame feels bad, while responsibility could feel good or bad depending on one's experience of it.

This "bad" feeling associated with blame and potentially responsibility can essentially be seen as a psychological injury. It is a disapproval or consequence that we want to avoid. Knowing what we know about people wanting to avoid pain and injury, it's really no surprise why so many people do not want to take responsibility and fear being blamed. This basic dynamic alone is enough to give you insight into why people behave as they do. And although knowing this can help you understand what's going on in the room, it doesn't actually help solve anything. People will still avoid blame and often avoid responsibility.

CHAPTER 2 – FACTOR 1: INTRODUCING BLAME AND RESPONSIBILITY

Example: Conflict Between a Married Couple

Let's look at this dynamic in action with an example of a conflict between a married couple. The wife feels that her husband is easily frustrated and quick to lose his temper. He often becomes verbally aggressive and difficult to communicate with. The husband feels that his wife is overly sensitive, blows things out of proportion, and tries to frustrate him on purpose.

The Background

The husband frequently becomes frustrated with his wife, as she makes nonsensical comments, does not listen to him, or respect his time. He finds that she is often the reason they run late for things, and no matter how many times he has raised it, the pattern continues. He finds her attention to her appearance prior to going out to be unnecessary and excessive, and no matter how many times he tells her she looks beautiful, this behavior continues. He has accepted her apparent need for an extensive wardrobe, expensive makeup, and a plethora of shoes but has never understood the need for it. Any one of these factors can easily anger and frustrate him, resulting in an outburst as he blames his wife's "fussing" for his frustration.

The wife often feels that her husband is unreasonable and harsh towards her, that he resents her for spending time on getting ready for events, that he hates her spending money on clothing and makeup and is unreasonably angry towards her. His outbursts create fear in her, and over time, she has come to dread that side of him. As such, she feels he disapproves of her and, by extension, does not feel comfortable or accepted by his family and friends. She finds herself constantly trying to find a way to be accepted by him, his friends, and family. This can lead her to tears or outbursts of her own.

The Scene

They are due to attend a family dinner and need to leave by 7 p.m. to arrive on time. It is now 6:45 p.m., and the wife has just come out of the shower. She has yet to do her makeup and decide which outfit to put on. The husband was ready 10 minutes ago and is pacing around the house, his stress building, anxious that they will be late yet again. The wife asks him to hand her something. He moves to help her, hoping this will get them to the event "less late." He trips over one of the shoes she left in the middle of the hallway. He stumbles and nearly twists an ankle. His stress has now turned to anger and rage, and he cannot contain himself any longer. He yells an obscenity at a now scattered pair of shoes and yells at his wife to hurry up because they are late. It's now 6:50 p.m.

The Husband's Perspective

Let's take a look at the husband's perspective of the events, keeping in mind this is all playing out in his thoughts, and his wife is not privy to knowing this. He feels pressured to be on time for the family dinner. His underlying belief is that it is rude to be late, or perhaps he feels it will reflect poorly on him. Others may think he is lazy, disrespectful, and not a man of his word, not to mention that he just wants to have a good time with his family. He was ready with time to spare and was ruminating about how his wife was once again the cause of their lateness. He even claims they *are* late, and although they likely will be late, they technically won't be late until 7:01 p.m. The importance of this is not the technicality but the fact that his mind has now taken a step towards blaming his wife and making that known to her.

His fixation on what is going wrong is leading him to become more stressed. He is also helpless (or seemingly so) in getting his wife ready in time. This stress and powerlessness lead to frustration and then, ultimately, anger directed at both his wife and some shoes. He has started to *Blame* his wife for their being late. And he feels justified in doing so.

His Failures

He may be correct in saying that his wife is delaying their departure and will likely cause them to be late. So, based on what he knows of the situation, it could be argued that his blaming her for this is justified, but is it helpful? And what has he failed to do?

CHAPTER 2 – FACTOR 1: INTRODUCING BLAME AND RESPONSIBILITY

Firstly, he has failed to consider why his wife is running late, but let's put this aside for a moment. He has also failed to take responsibility for his own emotions. He has allowed his frustration to lead to a lack of control over his emotions and has allowed some shoes and a clock to cause him to become aggressive towards his wife. Perhaps his underlying worry about what others will think of him is overriding the far more important matter of what his wife will think of him and how he is treating his life partner. He has also failed to take responsibility for looking where he was going. It's easy enough to blame her for leaving shoes in a hallway, but it is he who is responsible for his feet. His anxiety foundation is shaking, and rather than take responsibility to steady it, he has opted to blame his wife.

On a broader level, he has failed to remember the importance that his wife holds in his life and that his primary commitment should be towards her. As a result, he has been disrespectful towards her and their marriage. Perhaps ironically, his feelings or thoughts that she disrespects him by being late have led to him being disrespectful towards her.

The Wife's Perspective
Now, let's look at the wife's perspective, again keeping in mind that her husband is not privy to her thoughts at the time. She had been thinking about this dinner all week and wanted to put her best foot forward as she had never felt entirely accepted by his family. She had planned out her day to make sure she was ready on time, but she was held back at work, and then there was more traffic than usual on the drive home. When she did finally get home, she was in a state of anxiety, aware she was behind schedule, fearful that this would anger him and further perpetuate a pattern. This causes her to fumble things as she rushes to make up time.

Her anxiety foundation had been shaking all week. What she needed was the support of her husband to help calm her, make her feel accepted by him, and assure her that the family does accept her. But now, faced with his angry face and tone, she feels overwhelmed with anxiety. She feels anxious, scared, and alone. She thinks, "How am I going to make a good impression with your family when I'm too scared to sit next to you? I need you to be supportive and calm. I need an ally tonight so that I feel safe and can be at my best." This is what she felt, but not what she said. In fact, she has not communicated any of her concerns to him all week.

In her mind, she figures, at the very least, that she can look like a beautiful wife. This is why she buys the outfits and the makeup and why she takes so long to look *good enough* as a wife. She wants to look good for him and for his family, and he repays her by yelling and disapproving of her. She does not deserve to be yelled at, and it's not her fault he tripped over her shoes. Furthermore, he has not been very helpful, pacing around the house and making her more nervous. Her anxiety turns to anger, and she bites back to try and defend herself.

Her Failure

She may be correct in asserting that she should not be yelled at. It was not her fault that she was delayed, and if it had been, it would only have been due to her wanting to look her best and factors out of her control, such as work and traffic. She does not deserve such treatment, and she feels justified in standing up for herself and yelling at him. She would be right in not deserving to be yelled at, but is yelling in return helpful?

Arguably, her failure was that she did not communicate to him earlier that she was running late, nor did she inform him or prepare him for that eventuality as soon as she could. But this may have done little, if anything, to change the outcome and is ultimately not the core of the issue.

She has failed to take responsibility for her own emotions. She has allowed her insecurity to lead to a lack of control over her emotions and, subsequently, has allowed her desire to gain approval to cause her to be anxious all week. Just like her husband, her underlying worry about what others will think dominates her awareness of being a loved and accepted wife. Her anxiety foundation was shaking, and rather than take responsibility to steady it, she had been relying on him to steady it for her.

Both the husband and the wife are facing threats to their security. Both fear that others will judge them poorly, both have become anxious, both have failed to manage this anxiety, and both resulted in a "fight" response. Equally, both have failed to have a deeper conversation about what is happening to them. Given that he knows her propensity for running late, he could have raised this earlier and asked what he could do to help her during the day. Equally, she could have mentioned at the start of the week that she was anxious about the dinner and explained to him what she needed from him on the day.

In any case, the core issue here is a failure to recognize or stabilize their anxiety foundation and, equally, a failure to recognize their partner's anxiety and help them stabilize theirs.

The Underlying Dynamic

Both parties are turning towards "blaming" the other, with the wife perhaps also blaming herself to a degree. Both parties have, in their view, justified reasons to blame the other. The husband feels justified as he believes his wife is disrespectful, and she feels justified as he is being inconsiderate, not supportive, and now verbally abusive. However, blame, justified or not, is rarely, if ever, helpful.

It would be easy to argue for either side here, as both could attempt to justify their position. There is truth in the fact that the wife was running late, and there is truth that the husband was not considering his wife's needs. But viewing such a scenario in terms of who was wrong or who is to "blame" gets us nowhere. Blame serves only to cause shame in a person; it highlights their failings, and no one wants to have their failings put on display, especially not by the person whose love and acceptance you seek. Once blame is assigned, we will likely enter a negative exchange.

Keep it simple: Blaming your partner means injuring them, and as their partner, you are now responsible not only for causing the injury but also for supporting them while they are injured. To "win" an argument against your partner is to ensure your partner will "lose," which means your team, or your marriage, has just lost. There is no point scoring against your partner, only point scoring with them against what you face together.

The Solution

Should either party (and preferably both) have opted to take responsibility for themselves, they could have reduced their anxiety, stabilized their foundation, taken stock of the situation, and "chosen" how to respond to the situation. In this case, they were going to be late, and it no longer mattered why. All that matters now is how they manage the situation of being late, what state they will be in when they do arrive at the dinner, and whether their marriage is stronger or weaker as a result.

Unfortunately, when we are in a state of heightened anxiety, our ability to *choose* how to act is compromised. We tend to *react* rather than *act*, and this reaction is largely instinctual or at least trained in us from our early life experiences. Only when we reduce this anxiety do we have more choices about our actions.

If either of the parties had taken responsibility for themselves, then the argument may have been avoided. Had the husband taken responsibility for his own emotional state and expectations, then he would not have allowed himself to be verbally abusive towards his wife. Had he taken responsibility for looking where he was walking, he would not have tripped over her shoes, nor would he have then taken that out on her. Perhaps on a deeper level, had he taken on his responsibility as a husband to love and care for his wife, he would have opted to call his family and inform them they were running late rather than rush his wife and contribute to her stress.

On the other hand, had the wife, from an early stage, taken responsibility for running late, apologized to him, asked for his help, and explained why she was struggling to get ready in time, he *may* have been more understanding and realized she was not disrespecting him and his family, but that she was, in fact, anxious and in need of his support.

In truth, there are any number of things that could have been done by either party to reduce the chances of this conflict. Perhaps the wife could communicate better. Perhaps the husband could provide a safer environment for her to do so. Perhaps he could focus more on what was happening to his wife rather than being focused on what was happening to him. Perhaps she could have called him while in traffic to let him know she was running late. Perhaps he could then have called the family and said he or they were running late, showing support for his wife and reducing her anxiety. Had he been more aware of his wife's underlying anxiety, perhaps he could have spent the last week reassuring her that she was accepted by his family, or perhaps she could have worked through that underlying anxiety herself.

Keep it simple: Had he taken responsibility for his own anxiety and worked towards calming himself rather than venting his anger at his wife, then the argument could have been avoided. Equally, had she taken responsibility for her own anxiety, perhaps she would have felt confident in telling him she was running late and sought his help in supporting her to minimize how late they would be.

There are always any number of factors influencing a conflict, but ultimately, taking the path of responsibility rather than blame will inevitably reduce the negative impact on any interaction with a *reasonable* other. Always keep in mind that no one wants to be blamed due to your inability to take responsibility for yourself.

A General Rule

If all parties in any conflict can stop and take responsibility for their actions, then the conflict has its best chance of entering the resolution phase. It removes the anxiety of "What happened?" or "Who is to blame?" or, worse yet, "Am I going to be blamed?" and starts to create a safe environment or a resolution rather than fear. It places all parties into a state of realization of what they themselves need to improve on, leading them to be in a humbler state. Equally, they realize that everyone else is in the same state, which places all of them in a state of understanding and sensitivity rather than confusion or fear. The need for reality-checking has been satisfied, so their anxiety foundation steadies. Prior to responsibility being taken, each of them feels vulnerable to a degree, concerned that they may be footed with the blame. Now, with responsibility taken, this fear subsides, and they are relieved, grateful they won't have to enter a conflictual discussion. They perhaps feel a degree of gratitude to the other person, gratitude that they did not create a conflict and there is no longer any risk of being shamed. This makes everyone implicitly kinder to one another. As such, they are all likely to focus on what they can do to move forward while supporting one another in their own endeavors to move forward.

This is, of course, only when dealing with "reasonable" others. By reasonable, I am referring to someone who adheres to a typical and prosocial model of development. Or, more directly, I am referring to those who do not rate highly on the Dark Triad of personality types: narcissism, Machiavellianism, and psychopathy. When dealing with such people, or generally anyone who lacks empathy, then this dynamic of mutual care and consideration will often not apply. In fact, one should expect to be blamed, framed, or shamed when interacting with such individuals.

The above example looks at a husband-and-wife issue. But the same principles apply to any "relationship," intimate or otherwise. We see it within the work context between a boss and an employee. We see it within families, and we see it within friendships.

Keep it simple: When we feel blamed, we are likely to become defensive, which increases the likelihood of arguments. When all parties take responsibility for themselves, there is no need for blame to be attributed to anyone.

CHAPTER 2 – FACTOR 1: INTRODUCING BLAME AND RESPONSIBILITY

Barriers to Taking Responsibility

As we saw above, the solution to the problem is simple in theory: take responsibility for yourself, and you will not need to blame anyone else. This, in turn, prevents others from feeling anxious, as the risk of them being targeted or blamed has been removed. As a result, they are calmer, retain their clarity of thought, and function optimally. Your ability to take responsibility prevents others from becoming anxious and confrontational (recall that anxiety will result in fight, conflict, or flight), and it places you in a position of simply correcting yourself and moving on. This can, however, be psychologically difficult to do. It is common for people to struggle with this, as they may have some underlying defense to work through. Their history, or development, has taught them in one form or another that taking responsibility is psychologically risky. They may have developed a belief that admitting fault or taking responsibility will lead to greater punishment or harm to them. They may be trying to protect some sort of image they have for themselves, and, in their view, taking responsibility makes them look less capable or fallible in general.

For one reason or another, they have learned to protect or defend themselves from any potential psychological injury from others. Perhaps they want to ensure no one thinks negatively of them. They fear being disapproved of, insulted, branded incapable due to their error, etc. Others have developed a belief that taking responsibility is a weakness, while some may have experienced so much abuse that they can no longer tolerate any risk of negative appraisal, be it from others or from themselves. Whatever the reason behind the belief they hold, it can generally be summarized as "taking responsibility is dangerous and needs to be avoided." In any case, one's inability to take responsibility is a sign of a lack of psychological development. It must be said that this does not necessarily mean it is a sign of their lack of *capacity* for psychological development, but rather that they have not had sufficient opportunity or the right environment (teacher, guide, support) to learn how to take responsibility, and understand the value of it.

Inversely, only those who are psychologically resilient or well-developed will be forthright in taking responsibility. This is not to say that all well-developed adults will take responsibility all the time. Some may be very responsible for themselves; however, they will find certain scenarios too difficult and shy away from taking responsibility. We all have our weak spots.

Keep it simple: The inability to take responsibility for oneself is a sign of poor psychological development. It signifies one's inability to tolerate the potential negative appraisal should one take responsibility. This often stems from an insecure upbringing, which either taught insecurity or lacked appropriate encouragement and support.

We can liken this ability to take on responsibility (psychological development) to that of one's physical strength or physical development. If a person trains their body by lifting weights over an extended period of time, then they will be very physically developed. Subsequently, they have little problem lifting heavy objects, and the more developed they are, the heavier the object they can lift. But no matter how physically developed they are, they will inevitably come across an object they cannot lift. This is much the same for one's ability to take responsibility for themselves. How much responsibility they can tolerate over time, or how much responsibility they can take at any given moment, will depend upon how much they have trained or practiced doing so.

Let's take this analogy a step further: just like with physical development, some people are more genetically inclined to do better than others. We must consider this *possibility* in the realm of psychological development. Some individuals, be it due to their genetics, their temperament, their personality, or perhaps their intelligence, *may* have a greater capacity for psychological development. Furthermore, an athlete with exceptional physical development may sustain an injury that permanently reduces their physical ability from that point forward. Likewise, a person may sustain a significant psychological injury, which permanently reduces their psychological development from that point forward. These are all just considerations. I state them here so that people can keep in mind that they need to be working towards their own personal ability. The goal should be self-improvement or development (or helping our clients to improve) and not comparing ourselves to others, which could lead to becoming negative or setting unrealistic expectations.

The Training of Responsibility

Many of us have taken responsibility for something at some point, only to encounter others seizing the opportunity to "double down," reinforcing their point that we were at fault. Your taking responsibility was used as an admission of guilt, blame, fault, imperfection, etc. The child who says they are sorry for something, only to be met with the parent continuing to yell at them (likely due to the parent's own failure to take responsibility for their emotional state or contribution to the problem). The employee who took responsibility for making an error on the job, only for the boss to continue to dress them down or dock their pay.

Cases like these not only teach us *not* to take responsibility for our actions but also to actively avoid doing so in the future. Worse yet, it can teach us how to effectively blame others, so we are not held responsible, further perpetuating the blame game in a workplace, culture, or society. This teaches us to be *irresponsible* or responsibility-phobic, as we associate responsibility with shame and negativity rather than growth and positive development.

It also keeps us in a state of childlike development, where we fear consequences and attribute responsibility to negative consequences rather than growth. It prevents us from effectively developing into an adult. It could be said that adulthood can be measured by one's ability to take responsibility for oneself. As adults, we are expected to be accountable and responsible, whereas we do not reasonably expect this of a child. When a child tells a fib we not only see straight through it, but we also have a degree of understanding and forgiveness for it. We tend to gently correct the child, explain that we know the truth, and guide them softly to accepting what needs to happen to rectify the situation. If done properly, the child will learn it is safe to take responsibility and will come to learn the benefit of doing so in the long term. Ultimately, the child learns to take responsibility next time, and due to their history of being guided on how to rectify things, they now learn agency and a sense of pride in their ability to fix things.

However, when an adult attempts this childlike "fib" or lie, we do not have the same level of tolerance. We expect better of a grown adult and often become angered by their refusal to take responsibility. In essence, responsibility is a feature of adulthood. I would argue that at a psychological level, the primary distinction between children and adults is the ability to take responsibility for oneself. Just how "adult" someone is can be measured by how responsible they are, not how old they are.

Keep it simple: By taking responsibility for oneself, we remove the need to blame another.

Responsibility can be taught, and as with many things, it is best taught gradually during our childhood years. Placing too much responsibility on a child too soon can have a negative effect. It can rob the child of their childhood, which leads to other needs not being fulfilled. For example, it is well known that a young child should not feel responsible for protecting and providing for their family as it places them in a state of anxiety and undue responsibility. However, if we do not provide enough responsibility to a child over the course of their development, they are likely to not learn responsibility and, consequently, won't develop a healthy sense of agency or esteem.

Should we be in an environment where our caregivers and role models foster this gradual development of responsibility, we start to integrate responsibility into our personalities. We slowly become increasingly comfortable with the potential threat of a negative outcome and learn that, more often than not, taking responsibility works to our

CHAPTER 2 – FACTOR 1: INTRODUCING BLAME AND RESPONSIBILITY

advantage. The threat of our anxiety foundation shaking at the idea of being responsible will remain, but it will not be as dire. Our gradual acceptance of responsibility has taught us that even when anxiety strikes, we can stabilize and emerge stronger from the experience. This foundation of managing anxiety grows stronger with each challenge we face.

This process works best when there is adequate and early support from those caregivers. A young child will look to their parents for this support and will start to gauge their own anxiety/stability based on what they see in their parents. The parents' anxiety foundation is a point of reference for the child, so if the parents look stable, calm, and in control, then the child will get comfort and stability from this, regardless of their own anxiety foundation. The reverse is also true. An otherwise calm child can become very anxious at the sight of anxious parents. After all, copying is how children do most of their learning.

When children have a confident or stable example to guide them, their own self-confidence naturally grows. They do not fear trying new things or revisiting difficult things as they know they are safe in their attempts to do so. They assume that the activity is generally safe regardless of the outcome of the activity. Their anxiety foundation may shake slightly, but they are comfortable with this. They know it is expected and that it does not mean there will be a catastrophic failure in their house.

Again, this is comparable to physical development. If children are engaged in physical training that is appropriate for their stature, are encouraged by their caregivers and role models, are shown how to train, and see others do so without signs of anxiety, then they are likely to take a positive attitude to the task or at very least not fear it. Just as with physical training, sticking to it allows gradual improvement in both ability and confidence. Similarly, the psychological training of learning to take responsibility can lead to increased confidence and competence over time.

Ultimately, our upbringing, the lessons we learn, and the examples we follow greatly influence our development into responsible adults.

Children primarily learn through observation and repetition, making their early years pivotal in shaping their values and behaviors. This underscores the significant role parents play in shaping their children's future attitudes toward responsibility and accountability.

Keep it simple: Developing one's ability to take responsibility will be derived from ensuring they have enough self-esteem to tolerate the threat that taking responsibility poses.

Training Irresponsibility

This process of observing and replicating happens whether the person being observed is aware of it or not. This places children at risk of learning irresponsible behaviors because a parent or important other unintentionally models irresponsibility. Despite not intending to teach their child to be irresponsible, parents may unknowingly lead by example if they themselves haven't learned to take responsibility for certain aspects of their lives. An example of this might be when a parent consistently fails to tidy up after themselves and then scolds their child for not packing away their toys. The parent is inadvertently modeling undesirable and irresponsible behavior, then scolding a child for doing the same. This not only confuses the child but also teaches them they have failed, despite their very best effort to replicate the example set for them.

Failing to Teach

Another scenario where parents may unintentionally teach irresponsibility is when they miss opportunities to do so as they arise. In today's world, parents often feel overwhelmed by numerous demands and struggle just to get through the day, making it difficult for them to address issues in the moment. Often, they may find themselves repeating the same corrections well after the fact to "unteach" something.

Ironically, if parents had taken on their role and responsibility as the child's primary teacher when these opportunities first arose, they would likely have less corrective work in the weeks and years ahead. This is an example of teaching irresponsibility by failing to teach responsibility. It's not that parents actively want to teach their children to be irresponsible, but by failing to teach them how to be responsible, they do run this risk. This could be considered teaching irresponsibility by omission of responsibility. Unfortunately, this results in the child later being chastised for doing something wrong, and the parents scold the child for not taking responsibility, unbeknownst to them that the child had not been taught any different. The child is being held responsible for the parents' failure to teach. Is it any wonder they start to build animosity towards their parents in later years?

There are certainly instances where a parent simply assumes that the child should already know how to take responsibility for X or how to behave during Y, as though this is something that humans inherently know as they age.

Actively Teaching Irresponsibility

At first, it may seem difficult to comprehend why anyone would actively teach their child to be irresponsible. However, in cases where a parent has personally experienced fear or negative outcomes from taking responsibility in their own life, they may view teaching their child to avoid responsibility as a reasonable approach. Perhaps the parents are highly anxious and want to avoid conflict or responsibility out of fear, and so they pass this down actively. These parents do not intend to harm their children; they are simply teaching what they believe has been beneficial for themselves and what they think will similarly benefit their child. Unfortunately, they are simply not aware of the consequences of this teaching. They do not realize the value of taking responsibility, so they do not realize they are hampering their children.

Of course, there is a rare case where a parent intends to teach their child to blame others and escape responsibility. Perhaps the parent is narcissistic or sociopathic to some degree, and their approach to raising their children is to teach them how best to manipulate and evade.

Or perhaps, due to the nature of their environment, these are the skills that are most likely to ensure the child's survival.

Ultimately, we can be trained to either become responsible or irresponsible. This training can be direct or indirect and often subtle or by omission. Often, people are unaware that they are teaching a child something as they don't realize that children are constantly observing and absorbing, or they miss opportunities to teach their child something as the opportunity arises.

Learning by Experience

There are other ways for children to learn other than observation. They can often also learn from their own experiences with others, like a child who is shamed when they do take responsibility. They may well learn that taking responsibility is a wholly negative experience. They are not learning this by observing their parents, but rather learning by how they are treated by others or how they feel as a result of something.

Consider a scenario where a child breaks something in the house and takes responsibility for it, as they've been taught it's the right thing to do. If the parents respond by punishing the child excessively or equally to how they would if the child hadn't taken responsibility, the child may learn that there's no benefit in being honest and accountable. This is especially true if the parents fail to praise the child for taking responsibility or take the time to teach them why it was a good thing to do. The child is left with only the understanding that taking responsibility is emotionally or psychologically difficult, and it only results in equal or greater punishment than had they not taken responsibility. Overall, they learn that taking responsibility often leads to more negative outcomes than avoiding it altogether. In the future, they may be more inclined to not take responsibility and hope that they do not get found out. At least with that strategy, they have a chance of getting away with something, as opposed to a guaranteed negative outcome. In this case, while the parents have explicitly taught responsibility through their words, their actions unknowingly convey that there are no benefits to taking responsibility.

CHAPTER 2 – FACTOR 1: INTRODUCING BLAME AND RESPONSIBILITY

Keep it simple: Irresponsibility can be taught in a number of ways, often inadvertently. If our training teaches us how to effectively skirt responsibility, perhaps via casting blame on others, then we may grow to enjoy this feeling, and we are encouraged to continue this behavior. We learn that it is possible to get what you want or escape something you do not want without any consequences.

The Pleasure of Irresponsibility

Sometimes, this learning occurs internally, and parents may not be aware of it playing out. Let's take a basic example of a child stealing a cookie. Despite being told "no cookies before dinner," they succumb to their desire for the taste of the cookie and sneak one anyway. When the parents notice the missing cookie, and the child sees the anger on their face, they find a way to cast blame onto their younger sibling. The parents fall for the trickery and scold the younger sibling, believing they are justified in doing so. The older sibling knows how to deceive and, through this example, has learned that they can profit a cookie and successfully avoid any repercussions. It is a win-win in their young mind.

Furthermore, children may even come to feel a sense of pleasure or pride in their ability to deceive others, not necessarily out of malicious intent, but rather due to the immediate rewards such as getting a cookie or the thrill of successfully avoiding consequences. In any case, they learn that avoiding blame can result in getting them what they want without any negative repercussions. There may even be cases where the child feels a sense of superiority over their sibling or even their parent, as they rate themselves as "smarter" than the others.

The above shows how successfully avoiding responsibility can bring instant rewards. There is a benefit to doing this successfully, and so one can be encouraged to continue down this path. If allowed to grow in our early years, this instant reward, or instant gratification, that accompanies avoiding responsibility can become problematic.

Beyond childhood, there are many theaters that teach irresponsibility, and all of them come with their own "instant gratification." Adolescent life is littered with irresponsibility, and the fun of irresponsible behavior, along with the lack of consequence, often instills the "pleasure" of irresponsibility. The ways in which this can happen, and the sheer opportunity for it, is near limitless during this phase of life. A common example might be that of attending a party, drinking to excess, engaging in reckless but enjoyable activities, and having no consequences for this action. They have few, if any, financial commitments, so they can spend excessively on pleasurable substances. Their bodies are young and recover quickly from any physical consequences such as hangovers or even physical injury. Their peers often forgive or ignore bad behavior because they themselves are just as guilty of the same. There is often less regard for the opinion of their parents at this stage of life, or the parents may simply never learn of the events, so punishment is either scarce or absent. All in all, there is great scope for gaining pleasure from irresponsibility, with minimal risk of consequence. With so much instant gratification up for grabs and little to no cost, it's no wonder that many adolescents will take this route.

Instances of teaching irresponsibility also occur in adulthood, often in relation to some form of financial gain. Any number of jobs can teach a person to act recklessly, unethically, or otherwise immorally and then "manage the fallout" or avoid responsibility. Anyone who has observed any degree of "business" will be able to identify how frequently responsibility is avoided. Politics is an area where responsibility is often avoided and blame attributed. It is also seen in sales, finance, and the medical field. In fact, it can be seen in all industries that employ human beings. Although controversial, the reality is that many companies, if not all, are incentivized to avoid responsibility to avoid undue running costs. The fact that there are regulatory bodies of any sort suggests that there is scope for a company to behave irresponsibly. A basic review of human history will also quite shockingly show how common it is for people and companies to attempt to avoid responsibility for profit.

CHAPTER 2 – FACTOR 1: INTRODUCING BLAME AND RESPONSIBILITY

Often, the reward for avoiding responsibility is greater than the loss from getting caught. Unfortunately, this teaches adults and companies that being irresponsible is often worth the gamble.

Lies, cover-ups, and deflection are all commonplace and are done to avoid negative appraisal and, therefore, loss in general. Young professionals entering any field will observe their senior staff's behavior and come to realize that should they want to progress in that field, they should protect and ingratiate themselves with their seniors. Over time, they come to mimic their seniors and, as such, earn promotions and become those seniors. Hence, the culture of a workplace is propagated, often without the active realization of the individual that they are behaving as they are, especially if there is already a lack of responsibility taught at home.

As they invest more and more time into their careers—20, 30, 40 years—they consciously or unconsciously realize that they cannot risk losing that investment of time or money. When faced with a scenario where they have to take responsibility for a poor action, they instinctively avoid doing so. They have too much to lose and have spent those decades learning to do the opposite. They are inexperienced in taking responsibility but expert in avoiding it. It only makes sense to then play to your strengths!

On a psychological level, they are also unlikely to want to accept or admit to themselves or others that they are irresponsible or psychologically underdeveloped. They may believe that they are very psychologically developed, as they are so skilled at avoiding responsibility. They may well see this as a reflection of their intelligence and that they can outsmart others to convince them of an untruth; in some ways, this is true. They are well-developed in deception. I would argue that this is not healthy, deep psychological development but rather broad, shallow psychological development (broad in the sense of their broad development of deception, avoidance, etc.).

Some, however, do not take this cutthroat view and still believe that despite their actions, they are good, kind, decent, or reasonable individuals, viewing their actions as "just business." They square away their actions in the workplace or in their home with their partner or children and hold themselves to the belief that they are a good person. Or they are good in their "personal" life, while the rest is "just business." Furthermore, that behavior in the business sector is somehow excusable as that is how everyone operates. They normalize the avoidance of responsibility and justify it as part of the job. This can also play out in a marriage, where they normalize how they treat their partner and justify it as part of marriage.

Often, they justify their actions because the rest of their lives are now built upon them. The deception, blame, and capitalization over others in their work is what has funded their lives. It has brought them great pleasures or gratification in life. They enjoy the fruits of their avoidance of responsibility and are invested in protecting or justifying the behaviors that brought them that. To have to admit their life's work is built on the back of deception, blame, taking advantage of others, avoiding responsibility, and so on, would be to admit they have not acted as they themselves had hoped to. This can cause a crashing down of their identity, the equivalent of a hurricane hitting their psychological house while an earthquake hits their anxiety foundation. Such an experience is likely to be avoided at all costs.

This tactic of blaming others is done particularly well by narcissists, sociopaths, and otherwise skilled manipulators. The sociopath does this as a rite of passage, proving to themselves they are superior by weaving a web of lies, blame, and deceit, all while having you convinced that you are the problem. The more they succeed, the more their self-confidence and entitlement grows, and they carry on exploiting anyone they see as a viable target. The narcissist will have a desperate desire to convince themselves they are right, and by doing so, they get to protect their fragile egos and go on believing in their inflated sense of self. In my view, trying to develop a sense of responsibility in a sociopath is a fool's errand. In the case of a narcissist, there may be some instances of success, but it's unlikely to result in a long-term or consistent change.

Keep it simple: We avoid responsibility as it is an easier road with instant gratification. The cost of this, however, is a long-term reward, a sense of agency, and a genuine confidence in one's ability. Responsibility breeds confidence and long-term satisfaction.

The above examples are just some of the many ways that a person can grow to avoid responsibility. The danger of this is that responsibility often takes a degree of strength or emotional tolerance; it is psychologically difficult, just as physical training can be difficult. On the other hand, avoiding responsibility is an easier road, at least at the time. By avoiding responsibility, we get to avoid any psychological or emotional difficulty, much as sitting at home on the couch is easier than getting yourself to a gym and working out. Just as some choose not to engage in physical activity, some choose not to engage in psychological activity. Our world as it stands today does not require anyone to train physically. Equally, our world does not require anyone to train psychologically. I am not certain that people are even aware of psychological training; it seems the world does not reward it, and hence, little attention is drawn to its value.

Keep it simple: Taking responsibility comes with risk, and our anxiety can steer us away from it as we fear the short-term pain associated with it. But by doing so, we also avoid any long-term gain.

The Takeaway

Conflict tends to arise due to disharmony among the parties regarding what is really happening. Put another way, it is when there is a lack of agreed understanding of what occurred.

When there is uncertainty as to what has happened or is happening in a given environment or exchange, then anxiety is likely to rise as each person searches for answers in order to understand their environment. In the case of conflict, this is more likely to escalate if there is a lack of agreement as to what caused a given issue. This lack of agreement is often a result of someone, or multiple people, failing to take responsibility for their actions.

Once all parties take responsibility for their actions, the problem is well on its way to being resolved. Ironically, all parties want the problem resolved. However, one or more parties want it resolved without them being considered as part of the problem, so they avoid responsibility or, worse still, blame another for their own contribution to the problem. Should they have the "security" to take responsibility for themselves, then the remainder of the group would experience less internal conflict, and their admission would reduce the anxiety of others, which would lead to a cooperative approach to problem resolution. This is partly due to them not feeling blamed but also due to getting that sense of confirmation that their understanding of the problem was accurate, increasing their confidence in themselves and making them less likely to be aggressive.

The levels of irony do run deep in such an exchange. Simply put, taking responsibility requires a degree of maturity and security in oneself. Once responsibility is taken, then the conflict is on its way to a cooperative resolution, assuming the other parties are not so insecure as to need to shame the responsible party in a vain attempt to elevate themselves.

Keep it simple: If responsibility is taken, there is no need for blame. By avoiding blame, we avoid creating anxiety in others, which improves the likelihood of a cooperative resolution to the problem.

Chapter 3 - Foundations of the Blame and Responsibility Dynamic

What do we do to get on top of this dynamic? How can we understand it enough to avoid this trap, or how can we navigate it? Well, understanding how and why it exists can help you overcome it from your end. That is, understanding it can relieve you of the associated injury it can, and often does, cause. Knowing how to *navigate* it can help you respond to it differently and help *other* parties that are facing the potential psychological injury.

The Child–Adult Perspective

We can view blame and responsibility as two terms on the same continuum. Or perhaps as stages of development, with blame being an early stage of development or perhaps an undeveloped stage and responsibility being the developed stage. Simply put, blame is childlike, while responsibility is adult-like.

Blame

Consider the stereotypical example of a parent coming home from work. Their two 4-year-old children are standing in the living room next to a broken window, the offending ball lying on the ground in front of them. The parent asks, "Who did this?" The two children, seeing the parent's displeased face, quickly look at each other, then back to the parent, and simultaneously point at each other.

    Both children have gone through an unconscious process of self-preservation. Their little minds unconsciously and instantly understand that they need their parent's favor. They rely on the parent for their survival. The parent provides food, shelter, and emotional support, and without these things, they simply won't survive. So, they do the only reasonable thing they can: they blame someone or something else, in this case, their sibling.

This is, of course, flawed logic on the part of the 4-year-old. In most cases, a parent will not abandon a child over a broken window. A well-adjusted parent will only really be concerned about the safety of the child and look to make sure they aren't hurt. A less adjusted parent might yell at the children and chastise them for having broken a window; this may be due to the parent having their own underlying survival threats (such as being under financial hardship or lacking support of their own). A truly underdeveloped parent might yell, beat, shame, and otherwise psychologically injure the child.

In the first and second scenarios, the reality is that the parent is not going to abandon the child, and the child's survival is not under threat. In the second and third scenarios, there are at least threats to healthy development. However, the child cannot fully understand the parent's intentions. They are not able to completely decipher this. In the third scenario, though, a child quickly learns how dangerous a mistake can be and will tend to avoid making one.

Only in the final instance would this child be right in their logic of blaming someone else to ensure their own safety. However, this strategy of blame is the most effective in ensuring their own survival regardless of which type of parent they have; at least, it is the least risky strategy to employ. All they know for sure is that staying on the right side of the caregiver is a good idea. Why gamble with survival? By maintaining the approval of their caregiver, a child stands the best chance of surviving. This is, in fact, a functional and natural strategy for a 4-year-old.

The 4-year-olds intrinsically know that they do not have the financial or emotional resources to look after themselves. Children understand they need their caregiver for survival, so they must ensure their caregiver does not abandon them. Since they are not developed enough to look after themselves, they rely entirely on someone else.

CHAPTER 3 - FOUNDATIONS OF THE BLAME AND RESPONSIBILITY DYNAMIC

Therefore, they must seek their caregiver's approval at all costs.

It is also interesting to consider what the mind of a child is capable of and what it is not. I mention that they fear the parent's abandonment. I also mentioned that in most cases, the parent won't abandon their child over something so trivial (or at all); at least, it is not the parent's *intent* to abandon the child. Many parents forget that, unlike them, their child does not have much (if any) grasp on the concept of time. So, for a parent, sending the child to their room for breaking the window is little more than a mild punishment, perhaps just long enough for them to clean up the glass. However, for a child who has no concept of time, this is very much a form of abandonment. The child is already fearful of the broken window, then the look on the parent's face, and then the internal unconscious fear of abandonment and death. Then they are sent to their room, which very much translates to "You are being isolated, you will be on your own, and your parent/protector is displeased with you. There is nothing in that room that will give you safety other than the desperate hope that the parent comes to comfort you soon."

Although many parents are not planning to abandon their children, they often resort to rejecting their children when they are frightened. The child will learn this quickly, and as a result, they will learn to do what they can to avoid this. Be it lying, blaming, or starting to hold perfectionistic expectations of themselves to avoid getting in trouble in the future. The more we look at such situations from the perspective of the child, we start to see that in their worlds, these fears of abandonment are not that far off the mark.

Keep it simple: Children instinctively learn to use blame as a way of avoiding disapproval, which in their minds could lead to rejection, abandonment, and some form of death. Blame is born of fear due to the inability to survive on your own, and hence the need for the approval of others to maintain your survival. Developmentally, it is an inherently "childlike" strategy.

In summary, as children are not able to be self-sufficient in terms of financial, physical, and emotional needs, they are reliant on others for this. So, to ensure they can access these things, they need to retain the approval of those who can and do provide it, typically their parents. They require an adult to help them survive and provide for their physical and emotional needs. In fact, one of the key roles of the parent is to help develop the child's ability to regulate their emotions over time, something that starts with a great deal of supportive, affectionate care alongside education on what emotions are and how to manage them.

Children are not financially stable on their own, they are not emotionally stable without an adult helping to teach and regulate them, and they are neither physically safe (or stable) without the protection of an adult. So perhaps the simplest way to view this is that children are not physically, emotionally, or financially secure enough to look after themselves. Therefore, they have to blame others to ensure the favor of those who will provide these things for them. Only when they are developed enough, physically, mentally, and emotionally, do they no longer need these things from others, and they can move on from the use of blame as their survival strategy. Of course, this assumes that they do develop enough in these areas, as not all people do.

Keep it simple: Children are inherently insecure in themselves and blame others to maintain the favor of their carers to survive. Only when we become self-sufficient in the areas of physical, mental, and emotional ability are we able to consider moving past the blame strategy.

Responsibility

Now, having an understanding of why blame exists as a strategy and knowing that it is a perfectly normal, natural, and effective strategy for a child, we can start to look at how responsibility takes shape. The key here is to remember the primal drive of survival. Survival is what drives

CHAPTER 3 - FOUNDATIONS OF THE BLAME AND RESPONSIBILITY DYNAMIC

that 4-year-old to avoid disfavor by blaming someone else to ensure their survival. As we have seen, children are not capable of physically, emotionally, or financially supporting themselves. However, once someone *is* capable of ensuring their own survival or is not beholden to their parent or carer for this survival, then developmentally, they can progress from blame to responsibility. Let's take a look at this by developing the previous example.

The parent now comes home to their two 20-year-old children and a broken window. The parent asks, "Who did this?" The 20-year-olds look at each other, and one raises their hand and says, "It was me. Sorry, I'll get it fixed." (This, of course, isn't always going to be the way this scenario plays out, and we'll cover other variations later.)

This second scenario shows a 20-year-old who is able to take responsibility for their actions. This is only possible if the 20-year-old feels secure enough to manage the possible outcomes of taking responsibility. What it means to be secure enough will be a combination of the three factors we mentioned earlier: physical, emotional, and financial (or, more accurately, the ability to have sufficient resources without their survival being at threat).

A 20-year-old, or at least a reasonably developed one, is capable of acquiring resources to repair the damaged window, and therefore, they can take responsibility for that portion of the issue. In other words, they are financially secure enough to take responsibility. They need to feel physically secure enough to take responsibility, meaning they must feel capable of ensuring their own physical safety. By the age of 20, they are likely to no longer feel physically inferior to their parent or at risk of physical harm from them. They should also be emotionally secure or developed enough to tolerate and navigate any possible negative repercussions of their actions. For example, should the parent yell, abuse, shame, or insult them for breaking the window, the 20-year-old should be emotionally robust and stable enough not to have these things significantly impact their sense of self or general mental health should abuse or ridicule come their way.

Essentially, they can rely upon their own resources to survive and do not *require* their parents for this. That is, should they be abandoned, they can find work to ensure food and shelter or perhaps rely on friends, partners, or other family to assist them. Likewise, they have emotional strength and security of their own, so they do not feel inadequate or defeated due to a parent scolding them. Or perhaps they have enough emotional support from others to offset their scolding and, therefore, have the security to take responsibility.

As mentioned, this scenario does not always play out this way. Not every 20-year-old is financially and emotionally secure enough to raise their hand and take responsibility for their actions. Some are not secure enough in these areas and are at risk of not taking responsibility for their actions. If the 20-year-old has not gone through their development in a healthy and progressive way, they may well still be dependent on their parent's approval in order to feel "acceptable" or "good enough" as a person. If they have not developed a healthy sense of self and self-esteem and are relying on their parent's praise for their emotional security, then they are at greater risk of avoiding responsibility and continuing blame or avoidance.

Likewise, should the 20-year-old have sufficient fear that they will be removed from the home while also not having the capacity for financial independence for any reason, then they are also more at risk of not being able to take responsibility.

Keep it Simple: Blame is an insecure or childlike approach to managing conflict, failure, or an unfavorable event, while responsibility is a secure or adult-like strategy. One must have adequate security in themselves to be able to take responsibility. The level of responsibility will scale with their level of security in themselves.

CHAPTER 3 - FOUNDATIONS OF THE BLAME AND RESPONSIBILITY DYNAMIC

For someone to be able to take responsibility, they need to feel secure enough in themselves to do so. They need to believe that they are *physically* safe enough to do so. No one wants to admit to something if the accuser is likely to assault them for their admission.

They need to be *emotionally* stable or secure enough to face any possible emotional or personal attack for whatever they are taking responsibility for. This emotional stability is key and revolves around the person's level of self-esteem or identity. If they are secure in who they are and believe they are loved and accepted, or at least lovable and acceptable, they are likely secure enough to admit fault and take a hit to their self-esteem because it is solid enough not to be shattered. They may think, "This particular straw will not break the camel's back, so I will take it on and carry on." However, if they have a fragile ego or sense of self, a negative appraisal from another person might be too much for them to tolerate. It very well could be the straw that breaks the camel's back, so they avoid it. They cannot risk taking that responsibility and instead revert to blame or avoidance.

And finally, they need to be financially capable of taking responsibility for their actions, as some form of resources will be needed to resolve the problem and set things back in order.

Keep it simple: To take responsibility, one must be secure enough to do so. They must be secure in their ability to ensure their own survival. They need to be adequately developed physically, emotionally, and financially.

Complexities of the Dynamic

There are, of course, many ways the above three points of security (physical, emotional, and financial) could play out depending on a person's makeup. For example, someone may be so emotionally secure that they have absolutely no care of what others think. They may well take responsibility for breaking the window but have no desire to fix it. They would be willing to have others disapprove of them (or even disown them) for not addressing the problem. They are very willing to give up these people rather than pay for a window. By their judgment, it is a fair exchange, as they do not need or want the people for their survival. They don't feel any emotional need to address the aggrieved person's issue.

There is also the "Why don't you make me?" scenario. That means the person who breaks the window will take responsibility for it but feel so safe or superior that they won't be drawn to repair it. They respond with "Why don't you make me?" suggesting the other person is unable to make them address the grievance. In days past, this would have been a physical superiority factor. Perhaps today, that may also be a financial or intellectual superiority in that of being able to afford lawyers or "outsmart" the aggrieved party so as not to have to resolve the grievance.

Table 2: Blame/Responsibility Comparison

Blame	Responsibility
Childlike	Adult-Like
Insecure	Secure
Anxious	Confident

Chapter 4 – Blame and Responsibility: The Next Level

Thus far, we have looked at why someone will blame others or take responsibility for themselves and how this is related to their levels of insecurity and security. Those who are insecure will blame, which is a childlike or limited development state, while those who are secure will take responsibility, which is an adult-like or good development state. This foundational understanding of the Blame-Responsibility Dynamic is enough to often identify why there is a conflict between two or more people. Conflict will often arise when someone fails to take responsibility for themselves or starts blaming others.

The relationship between blame and responsibility can be complex, especially in a dynamic between two people. Each person may tend towards either blame or responsibility and if they blame, it could be directed at the other person or themselves. To help resolve a conflict, we need to identify which approach each person is taking. If either is focused on blaming, finding a fair resolution will be challenging.

To better understand how to go about resolving conflict using this Blame-Responsibility Dynamic, we first need to put forward a model to help identify or categorize how a person fits within it. To do this, I propose three layers to help better understand the dynamic as a whole. Importantly, these layers are not necessarily entirely distinct from one another and are presented more as a guide toward understanding.

Layer 1 looks at how a person responds based on what *they themselves* have done. When they make an error, do they tend towards taking responsibility or assigning blame to another? This layer has been discussed in earlier chapters and tends to suffice for identifying the Blame-Responsibility Dynamic in simple exchanges.

Layer 2 looks at how things play out when this direction is reversed. That is to say, when making an error, do they tend to blame themselves or assign responsibility to others?

Layer 3 introduces the idea of how a person responds when *someone else* makes an error and how their tendency is to blame themselves or take responsibility for the error regardless of who is responsible for the error.

Layers 2 and 3 become more important when looking at individuals who have more complex profiles, such as those with childhood neglect or trauma, as well as those with personality disorders.

One could argue for a fourth layer, in that when someone else makes an error, does the person tend to accurately hold that person responsible and not take responsibility for the other's mistakes? However, by and large, this is what you would expect from someone who is well-functioning or simply willing not to comment or engage with others seeking to draw one in when they make an error.

Table 3: Layers of the Blame-Responsibility Dynamic

Layer	Blame Tendency (Childlike)	Responsibility Tendency (Adult-like)
1 – Own Error	The Blamer (of others)	The Responsible (self)
2 – Own Error	The Self-Blamer (self)	The Avoider (others)
3 – Others' Errors	The Self-Blamer	Overly Responsible

The second and third layers provide for more complex dynamics, as they consider what seems to be the less logical approaches of blaming self and taking responsibility for others. I say they are less logical as they appear to be contrary to the "survival" paradigm underlying this dynamic. Despite this, there is a logical reason for these strategies, which we will explore throughout this chapter.

Layers 2 and 3 can have some overlap and are only listed separately in an attempt to provide more structure. Layer 2 brings in the variation of the "Self-blamer" and the "Avoider" of responsibility, while Layer 3 brings in the "Overly Responsible," which arguably is just an overly active variation of the "Responsible" type in Layer 1. These layers should not be taken as levels of complexity or pathology but rather a system to gradually introduce the ways that this Blame-Responsibility Dynamic can develop in people. The list below provides a brief introduction to each of these variations, with more detailed explorations to follow.

- **The Blamer** - A person who tends to blame others rather than take responsibility for their own actions.
- **The Responsible** - A person who takes responsibility for their own actions rather than getting caught up in blaming.
- **The Self-blamer** - A person who will tend towards blaming themselves regardless of who may be at fault.
- **The Avoider** - A person who tends to avoid any responsibility taking of their own, and expertly engineers the narrative to frame others as the responsible party. They have learned to avoid negative language, which would reveal them as "The Blamer," but at heart, the Avoider is essentially a creative, articulate blamer.
- **The Overly Responsible** - A person who takes on responsibility not only for themselves but also for others. This strategy could be either positive or negative, depending on the circumstances.

Here we are adding three new variations to the two that were introduced in the previous chapter, leaving us with five basic "types" of people when it comes to the Blame-Responsibility Dynamic. As stated earlier, blaming, in general, can be viewed as a childlike, insecure, or underdeveloped strategy, whereas taking responsibility is considered an adult-like, secure, or well-developed strategy. This holds true with the introduction of the Self-blamer, Avoider, and Overly Responsible. However, we will see how adult-like or secure strategies can have their own potential problems.

The Blamer

I alluded to the Blamer in the previous chapter. This is the individual who failed to develop a stage of security in themselves where they cannot tolerate disapproval or criticism. They tend to take comments from others very personally and are sensitive to criticism, perhaps even finding criticism where there was none. As such, they develop a tendency to become defensive or are quick to deflect blame onto others. This is done to protect the ego, to protect themselves from "being wrong" or having "done wrong."

This is essentially the same drive that we saw in the example of the young child in the previous chapter. The child fears disapproval from their mother, assuming it means she will no longer love them, will abandon them, and it will ultimately lead to their death. The Blamer also has this same mindset. They may not consciously believe that they will be abandoned and die, but unconsciously, this thought process is playing out. On a conscious level, they may simply understand that they want to be liked or not want to be disapproved of.

However, their psychology plays out the child-level thought process of disapproval = unlovable → abandoned → death. Even though a disapproving or angry mother is unlikely to resort to abandoning their child, that is not understood by the child. Should the child fail to be taught that they will not be abandoned, or worse still, led to believe they will be abandoned, then this tendency to blame in order to survive can remain throughout one's life. Hence, a Blamer type is born.

There are those who would conclude, or assume, that all Blamers are narcissists. In my view, this is not accurate. Although it is true that narcissists are often Blamers, not all Blamers are narcissists. The narcissist and the blamer share the trait of blaming others and lacking true security. However, a narcissist also holds other key traits that the everyday "Blamer" does not. For example, the narcissist will genuinely have no empathy for the other party and not concern themselves with any harm they do. They see themselves as superior to others. The Blamer, on the other hand, does not necessarily hold this view; they are likely unaware of their blaming nature or why they have it. They are not necessarily trying to be hurtful to others and may be genuinely remorseful in the aftermath. They simply have not developed the self-esteem (strength, worth, value, independence, etc.) to be able to "risk" taking responsibility for themselves and have fallen into a long habit of blame.

Keep it simple: The Blamer type arises from the natural childhood fear of abandonment and death having never been sufficiently soothed. By lack of a sense of safety, childlike thinking is never truly dispelled. The child learns (quite adaptively to the environment) that admitting fault or taking responsibility leads to isolation, abuse, and emotional danger. As such, they learn to blame others rather than take responsibility for their own actions.

The Responsible

The Responsible type was also alluded to in the previous chapter and is self-explanatory: it is the individual who takes responsibility for their actions once it is evident that it is their responsibility to take. I make this distinction of "once it is evident" as even a well-developed and highly responsible person is not necessarily all-seeing. Once they see that their action leads to an issue, they take responsibility and set about resolving the issue.

These people have, over time, developed a healthy sense of self. They have learned that taking responsibility will not lead to abandonment and death, even though they shared that same mindset in early childhood. Whether through parenting or life experiences, they learned that mistakes do not lead to abandonment (at least not most of the time) and that as they grow physically, mentally, and emotionally, they can come to rely on themselves to resolve issues. Often, they will have had a guiding light in that of parents or significant others who have displayed this for them. For example, a parent who identifies their own mistake and how to go about resolving it or a parent who meets the child's admission of guilt with love and acceptance rather than abuse and rejection.

An example of this might be when the child breaks a window, the parent cuddles them, comforts them, ensures they are safe and unharmed, then asks what happened, encouraging the child to come clean and continuing to show love and concern for the child. As opposed to asking who broke the window from a distanced standing position looking down on the child, only to then yell insults at them for their stupidity and send them to their room, alone, without any emotional safety, ultimately proving the child's fear of disapproval → abandonment to be true.

Keep it simple: The Responsible type arises from a safe environment that fosters growth and age-appropriate responsibility taking. This leads them to grow in their self-esteem/belief and dispels their fears of responsibility-taking.

The Self-blamer

Thus far, we have discussed the basic foundation of this dynamic and how we tend to blame others when we lack the security to take responsibility for ourselves. This dynamic is common and often appropriate for children as, in many cases, they are not capable of, nor should be expected to, take responsibility for themselves. We also touched on how well-adjusted adults are able to take responsibility for themselves rather than blame others because they have developed that sense of security within themselves.

However, there are cases where people *blame* themselves rather than take responsibility for themselves or blame others. This blaming of oneself is distinctly, but sometimes subtly, different from taking responsibility for oneself, and there are a number of underlying thought processes as to why someone might become "The Self-blamer." The

CHAPTER 4 – BLAME AND RESPONSIBILITY: THE NEXT LEVEL

Self-blamer can develop in a number of ways, but ultimately, it is considered a generally unhelpful approach regardless of the underlying reasons behind it. The list below breaks this down and gives an overview of why someone may opt for this self-blame approach rather than the typical Self-blamer or Responsible type.

1. Blame self rather than hold self responsible (View self negatively)
2. Blame self rather than hold others responsible (Martyr, protector)
3. Blame self rather than let others blame you (Defensive, fearful strategy)
4. Blame self rather than let others hold you responsible (Demoralized)

By looking at each of these variations, we can come to a better understanding of why a person would enact them and what they tell us about their self-image or view of the world they live in. From a self-help perspective, this can help you understand which strategy you might be enacting and why. For the therapists out there, it can provide a structure for your understanding of clients and hence assist with planning how to approach or continue with your clients.

1. Self-blame over Self-responsibility: The Defeatist or Negativistic Strategy

It may not be immediately obvious where the difference is between self-blame and taking responsibility. The defining feature between them is the person's view of themselves, which often becomes apparent in the language they use and the emotion behind the moment.

Those blaming self will invariably use negative language towards themselves. They may believe they are simply taking responsibility for themselves; however, the negative language they use shows a negative self-image or even disdain they hold for themselves. This is not something you will see in those who take responsibility. For example, they may state: "Oh, that's my fault. I'm such an idiot," or "I should have known better. I messed that up, typical."

This is accompanied by a sense of hopelessness, defeat, or expected failure on their part. Rather than the ownership and acceptance that one would see in the Responsible type, the Self-blamer is far more likely to take the matter personally (or personalize the matter) and have it negatively shape their "self-esteem" or image. On the other hand, the "responsible" person would not have this negative self-appraisal. The responsible person would accurately be able to identify the negative outcome of any given event, but they would not take this outcome personally or attribute it to who they are. The responsible person takes it in a more "professional" way, in that they identify the issue, accept they caused it or are responsible for it, and set about solutions. They have an inherently more positive or objective mindset.

The Self-blamer will start to identify as a person who always makes mistakes, who will never be good enough, and who is expecting to fail again. Furthermore, they often expect to be blamed for things in general. They have become accustomed to "getting it wrong" and they fall in with that belief structure. This is then confirmed in their mind the next time something goes wrong. Conversely, the responsible person does not attribute the mistake or error to themselves but to the action they took (or didn't take). As such, they can choose to take a different action next time. Herein, the responsible person identifies themselves as someone who can and does change and as someone who improves; hence, they do not attribute negativity to themselves.

Keep it simple: The Self-blamer likely has a negative self-concept, personalizing a negative result. This differs from a responsible person, who does not attribute the negative outcome to themselves but rather to their chosen action, an action that can be changed in the future.

An important note here is that a responsible person will admit fault without innately attributing fault to their character or personality. They understand the fault was due to their action, not their identity. The Self-blamer fails to make this separation, and as such, they come to believe they are the error. Therefore, they are at greater risk of low self-esteem as they form the belief they are not "good enough."

Here are some examples of how to identify Self-blamer talk compared to a responsible adult.

The Self-blamer:
- "I can't believe I did that. I'm so bad at this; it would have gone better without me."
- "Oh, that was my fault. Sorry, I keep getting this wrong."
- "I kept fumbling the ball. I'm so bad at this game. I'm the reason we keep losing."

The Responsible adult:
- "Sorry, that was my fault. It's okay, I've got this now."
- "Yeah, that was me. I should have done better. I'll get onto that and get it back to you."
- "I kept fumbling the ball today. I'm not sure what's happening today, and I'm clearly not at my best. I'm going to put in some more practice before the next game."

As we can see, the primary difference here is that of not personalizing the mistake and having some view towards improvement or a solution. The Self-blamer tends not to view the situation as improvable. They may know that it can be improved or could be convinced of it, but their instinctual mindset takes them towards the negative.

As a result of this mindset or belief, the Self-blamer is highly prone to having low self-esteem, and the very act of self-blaming will erode one's esteem and confidence. Over time, this leads to having no confidence and a great deal of anxiety and will often lead to depression. It's an inherently *de*structive mindset and often leads to a "self-fulfilling prophecy."

The responsible adult has a more accurate, measured, and positive approach to admitting fault and taking responsibility for their actions. They are more balanced in that they acknowledge their contribution to the issue and then back themselves in their attempt to resolve the issue. Their internal dialogue (or self-talk) is not overly negative; they have some degree of confidence or belief that they can resolve the issue or improve over time. They do not take the issue as a reflection of who they are or who they are destined to be forever.

Keep it Simple: We can summarize the Self-blamer as one who has a negative self-view and is prone to low self-esteem. Their strategy is destructive to their own development.

2. Self-blame over Holding Others Responsible: A Protective or Martyrized Strategy

This is perhaps the least common variation of self-blaming. In this variation, the person blames themselves before the person at fault can take responsibility for themselves. There may be a range of reasons for adopting this strategy, but the two most common or logical ones are wanting to protect someone from potential fallout and having been conditioned to self-blame (possibly due to being raised by an avoidant/blaming or narcissistic/sociopathic parent).

2a) In the case of someone looking to self-blame in order to "protect" another.

The underlying motive here is typically to step in and "take one for the team." It's the case of one person choosing to not just take responsibility for someone else but take responsibility and amplify it with the negative flavor of blame. In this case, the self-blamer will color their admission with negativity, perhaps to ensure the spotlight is firmly off the person they are seeking to protect or to ensure the other person feels entirely absolved of the responsibility.

Typically, the self-blamer in this scenario knows they are not to blame. Their primary motive is that of protecting the other. However, there may be scenarios in which a person has become a pathological self-blamer and no longer recognizes or values who is responsible. They may believe they are acting to protect another, but there may also be a martyr-type drive behind their actions. In any case, whether they realize it or not, they place greater value on the other person than on themselves. Be it consciously or unconsciously, they have decided that they are of lesser worth than the other and hence have put themselves in the firing line to save the other.

One such person or archetype that might take this self-blaming role is the "protective mother." This is the case of a mother stepping in to ensure her child does not have to face any potential consequences of taking responsibility. Again, considering that her response is up for debate, it may be an instinct, a case of idealizing her child, or a learned strategy due to circumstance. In any case, she is driven to protect her child. This protection could be helpful in shielding her child from potential injury, or it could be harmful in that it prevents them from developing a sense of responsibility and the inevitable confidence that would come of that.

In the case of this mother being overly protective and never allowing her child to take responsibility, she may believe she is protecting them from potential harm when, in reality, she is preventing them from growth and development. She may idealize her child, feel they can do no wrong, or simply never want them to feel any emotional pain, so she ensures she puts herself between them and any responsibility. Unfortunately, this leads to an underdeveloped individual. The child is less likely to ever learn to take responsibility and hence remain in the child and blame mindset well into their adult years, or perhaps forever. Terms that are synonymous with those who have never had to take responsibility include spoilt brat, man-child, diva, or even narcissist. Next time you come across a chronological adult who never takes responsibility for their actions, consider how they came to develop in such a way.

There are, of course, situations where this "protective mother" *is* acting in the child's best interest. For example, take a situation where the child has broken something in the house, and the violent, abusive, drunk father comes home. The mother, being aware that her husband will undoubtedly physically abuse the child if he learns the child is responsible for the damage, may well opt to self-blame rather than allow her child to take responsibility. Again, this is a horrible but unfortunately realistic situation. Of course, the ideal outcome here is that the abusive man takes responsibility for his own actions and does not resort to any form of violence or abuse. However, with the mother knowing full well this won't happen, she opts to put her child's safety before her own.

Keep it simple: Attempting to protect others from responsibility by taking blame runs the risk of eroding your own self-worth while preventing others from developing a sense of responsibility and adulthood.

2b) In the case of someone who has been conditioned to self-blame

In psychology, the term "conditioned" means to train a certain behavior into or out of a person or animal. This is perhaps best illustrated in the hallmark study by Pavlov referred to as the "Pavlov's dogs" experiment, wherein he would ring a bell just prior to serving dogs food. The presence of the food naturally stimulated salivation in the dogs, and by consistently ringing the bell in association with the food, the dogs learned to associate the sound of the bell with food. As a result, over time, when Pavlov rang the bell, the dogs started to salivate regardless of whether or not he brought them food. This hallmark experiment is a representation of "classical conditioning." It shows how we can control an animal's actions or behavior by manipulating some factors. This "classical conditioning," or more simply "conditioning," is just as prominent in humans as it is in dogs.

Unlike the scenarios above, where a person is looking to protect someone by self-blaming, there is also the unfortunate case where someone has been "conditioned" to self-blame. Much like a dog has unconsciously been trained to salivate at the sound of a bell, some people have been unconsciously conditioned to self-blame in the presence of a given stimulus, such as conflict or aggression.

Take the instance of a person having had past experiences wherein they were made to believe they are at fault when they are not. Perhaps they have a history of a narcissistic partner or parent. They have been conditioned by them to self-blame. Essentially, the self-blamer here was repeatedly taught that they were at fault whenever there was any conflict. Just as the dog's salivation was triggered by the bell rather than the reality of there being any food, the Self-blamer self-blaming is triggered by any "conflict" rather than the reality of being in the wrong. They simply assume that if there is conflict, they should blame themselves or perhaps risk being abused as they were by their narcissistic or otherwise unhealthy parent or partner of the past. Even though they are now free of these damaging relationships, they carry it forward into future relationships or just general day-to-day life. They now instinctively blame themselves at every turn. When faced with a scenario where a responsible other person is poised to take responsibility for their own actions, this self-blamer will instinctively step in to blame themselves even though it was not called for.

Keep it simple: One can be conditioned to self-blame, essentially being trained to believe they are the cause of all problems. They adopt this role of being at fault and step in to blame themselves to avoid the abuse of not doing so.

---

3. Self-blame Over Being Blamed: The Defensive or Fearful Strategy

Another variant is that of someone blaming themselves before anyone else gets a chance to blame them. This can occur regardless of who is at fault or in error. For example, the self-blamer may be at fault and realize this, and so they will blame themselves before anyone else can blame them. The self-blamer may *not* be at fault; however, they are expecting to be blamed by someone, so they self-blame before this can happen. This variation can only really play out when there is a lack of the Responsible type involved. It's a case of what can happen when there are only blaming types involved.

Essentially, this is the "Get out ahead of it" strategy but with a blaming tone rather than the typical "taking responsibility" tone. If a person knows or expects to be blamed for something, regardless of who was at fault, they will get in first and blame themselves for it. It is an attempt to minimize the blow to themselves by not letting someone else point the finger at them.

Self-blame before being blamed is again common in those who have an underlying sense of low self-esteem, a history of being blamed, or both. It is commonly seen in those who have had the misfortune of being in an emotionally manipulative or abusive relationship. Their partner, employer, or perhaps culture has repeatedly blamed them for things that may or may not be their fault, and over time, they come to expect to be blamed. In some cases, they believe they are to blame; in others, they simply accept that they are the scapegoat and accept the blame regardless of fault. In any case, they have learned that if they blame themselves first, then the immediate emotional pain is less than it otherwise would be. If they step in and blame themselves, they can do so with slightly less negative impact than they should if they wait to take the brunt from someone else. They may have to ensure that they are adequately scathing of themselves to satisfy their abuser, or they risk the abuser adding to the blame even after they have already attributed it to themselves. There may be a degree of empowerment on the side of this particular Self-blamer in that, at the very least, they can control their action by blaming themselves. However, it is poor compensation for the damage it sustains. It is a truly horrid dynamic, but sadly, one that does exist, particularly when dealing with highly insecure individuals (in reference to the abuser) or narcissists (again, in reference to the abuser).

This Self-blamer has essentially learned or been trained to self-blame. They take it on as a survival strategy to minimize the damage from an abusive person or environment. "Get in first; it hurts less than being blamed by them" is the mindset here. This self-blame strategy may, in fact, mitigate the emotional pain at that instant. However, prolonged and persistent instances of this can lead to long-term emotional damage. The repetition of negative self-appraisal can lead that mindset

CHAPTER 4 – BLAME AND RESPONSIBILITY: THE NEXT LEVEL

towards "I deserve this" and becomes highly destructive to their esteem. They become convinced they deserve such treatment and that they are always to blame. This starts to become a big part of their self-image. It is a terrible blend of attempted self-preservation in the moment but ensuring self-destruction over time.

On an individual level, this dynamic is often seen in partners of sociopaths or narcissists. The constant criticism from their partner effectively trains them to accept blame and then self-blame. It can be seen in individuals and groups of people in "toxic" or abusive workplace environments (or cults). The boss or "leadership" will systematically lay blame at the feet of the subordinates, who are in no position to argue or contest the leadership's statements due to fear of loss of employment or ejection from a group. Over time, they lose their sense of self. They expect daily criticism and learn to believe they are not enough or deserve blame. It can also occur in massive populations of people in certain cultures or tyrannical dictatorships, such as slave populations or citizens of oppressive regimes. The insecure or sociopathic "masters/leaders" persistently blame them for any ill. Over time, the citizens may even start to agree with their overlord, perhaps out of being purely conditioned to do so, learned helplessness, or some twisted belief that it will bring them favor.

Keep it simple: When a person has come to expect being blamed for everything, they may resort to self-blaming. This strategy could be a result of conditioning or a belief that it is less harmful than the alternative. Over time, this strategy can and often does erode one's confidence and create a negative self-belief. It is a very disempowering dynamic.

---

4. Self-blame Over Being Held Responsible: The Demoralized

Similar to variation three, this individual will jump to self-blame, likely due to a strong negative self-identity or at least a belief that they are always "at fault." They do not take responsibility or allow others to hold them responsible as they are only familiar with the more negative approach of blame. It is likely that they have been conditioned to simply blame themselves for any mistake rather than knowing there is a more positive and constructive method of *responsibility*. They may well see being held responsible as the same thing as blaming themselves. In all likelihood, this is due to never having been taught the potential positive outcomes of responsibility and only ever taught the negative approach of blame.

Ultimately, this type of self-blamer has a mindset similar to that in variation three, as they simply do not recognize the difference between being held responsible and being blamed. Therefore, they only foresee being blamed and play things out as those in variation three.

Keep it simple: The root of this "self-blame before being held responsible" is overcompensation and is based on some underlying belief that they are "not good enough" or "always to blame" and deserve the negative skew of blame rather than the measured and more neutral tone of responsibility.

Pointing Out Self-blame

It's possible that others will not notice the difference between someone self-blaming versus taking responsibility for themself. People may not notice or will not voice that they notice a person is taking a negative tone rather than a more positive, *responsible* tone. The more sensitive or caring individuals may take the time to raise this with the Self-blamer, and with enough support and retraining, this issue can be improved upon and even resolved over time. However, these Self-blamers can equally be targeted and taken advantage of by those looking to avoid responsibility of their own. Even the well-intentioned who would like to help or correct the Self-blamer may instead choose to keep quiet to not bring themselves into the spotlight or even not want to face the Self-blamer's disagreement with them on the topic.

In an instance of two co-workers in conflict, the Self-blamer here is unlikely to be corrected into "self-responsibility" as the co-worker is likely more preoccupied with their own survival in the conflict. They are relieved not to be to blame and may not have the presence of mind to guide their co-worker away from blame and into responsibility. On the other hand, the example of a well-balanced (and rested!) parent may well identify their child speaking negatively about themselves and correct this towards responsibility rather than blame. A therapist should identify this self-blame strategy and correct it with their client.

How Does One Become a Self-blamer?

A primary cause of developing a self-blame mindset is that of early childhood learning. Should a child be blamed by others rather than supported and taught how to take responsibility, then they are likely to develop such a mindset. Those who fail to make achievements throughout their development or fail to have their achievements recognized are also at risk of developing a negative self-image that can lead to becoming a Self-blamer. This is a mindset that can spiral over time. A child who is blamed and starts to identify as "always wrong" is then more likely to accept such treatment from others as they move into adolescence. They are more likely to believe a teacher who blames them and accept friends who do the same. This is because the views of these teachers and friends are in line with what they expect from themselves. Hence, it's "a language they understand" and therefore accept. This then places the person at risk of selecting or accepting a partner that mimics this same narrative, and so the mindset and dynamic with others is perpetuated across their lives.

Self-blamer Mindset

The mindset of a self-blamer is inherently negative, which is to say they think negatively of themselves. Anxiety is also very often present, as negative self-appraisal and anxiety are commonly seen together. When they enact self-blame, a degree of psychological self-destruction occurs. There is a litany of possible ways in which they can do this, but ultimately, they are working on the presumption that they are "not good" or "not good enough," and should something go wrong, it is likely their fault. As a result, they either consciously or unconsciously believe that others are superior or more valuable than themselves, which reinforces their belief that they are not good enough. This pattern invariably erodes their self-esteem, influencing their actions in life and interactions with others, which often further reinforces their self-belief. The longer this cycle of behavior continues, the greater the risk of developing issues such as anxiety and depression.

Unfortunately, this mindset is, at times, perpetuated by others. There are some who notice this pattern in a person and realize that they can benefit from it. These are often the "irresponsible" types, who will use such a person to offload their responsibilities or otherwise keep them down to feel superior to someone. In truth, those who prey on the Self-blamer have deep-seated issues of their own, and they avoid or hide these issues by casting negativity onto the Self-blamer. Adding more dysfunction to such a scenario is that the Self-blamer often accepts and maintains such a person in their life, not because they enjoy the emotional abuse, but because it is in line with their own internal self-belief that they are lesser than others. And so, an incredibly unhealthy co-dependent relationship is formed.

Summary: Self-blamer

As demonstrated in the scenarios above, this self-blame strategy consistently ends in some form of pain or injury to the Self-blamer. In some situations, a Self-blamer may act to protect others, but in other cases, this attempt at protection can lead to longer-term damage or "underdevelopment."

The Self-blamer runs the serious risk of continuing to erode their self-esteem as they consciously or unconsciously place their worth beneath others. Should the Self-blamer persist, they place themselves at risk of developing a sense of worthlessness, which in turn puts them at risk of high levels of anxiety and depression. Simultaneously, they are running the risk of preventing the other person from developing the ability to take responsibility for themselves and stunting their development into adulthood.

The Avoider

As the name suggests, the Avoider will avoid any form of responsibility or blame. While they share the trait of not taking responsibility with the Blamer, the Avoider differs in that they don't actively "blame" others. Instead, they avoid acknowledging or addressing the issue altogether. By changing the topic or denying the problem, they hope to evade both the issue and any associated responsibility.

On a basic level, the Avoider will simply stay quiet, much like the spouse who pretends not to hear their partner struggling with some domestic chore. They remain quiet and still in the hopes that their struggling partner does not notice them, knowing that their partner is too "kind" or "proud" to ask for help directly. When facing more significant issues, the Avoider will resort to clever use of language or physicality to deflect or minimize the issue. Often, they will have a set of go-to skills for this deflection and minimization, perhaps humor to minimize or affection to deflect and change the topic. Anger could also be used to send a message, not to push them for fear of an outburst. Alternatively, they may use some clever, albeit inaccurate, logic to minimize and deflect the conversation towards something else entirely. There are many examples of these sorts of tactics. In some cases, they are legitimate tactics used to try and lighten the mood and bring the issue into perspective. However, if used persistently or disproportionately to the situation, they become an avoidant tactic. Following are some examples of the Avoider's tactics.

The Silent Avoider

This is the person who ignores the issue, says nothing, flies under the radar, and hopes that the other party forgets, moves on, and does not have the courage to make a direct accusation or some other such thing that allows them to avoid it with minimal effort.

The Joking Avoider

This is the person who will constantly use humor. When used in appropriate situations, this is a very effective and healthy approach as it prevents an issue from blowing out of proportion. However, when used constantly, it shows the Avoider's inability to recognize the seriousness of a situation and the negative impact that their humor is now having. It falsely assumes that humor cures or resolves everything, and it prevents them from taking on responsibility and ultimately developing as a person. This is perhaps the "nice guy" who never grew up, the person who learned that humor worked well to avoid taking responsibility but never learned how to handle serious or significant situations. They never learned that their ongoing use of humor was leaving others to take on the responsibilities they themselves failed to, and by virtue of this, they never learned the benefits of growth and self-development that come from taking responsibility.

The Skilled Avoider

This flavor of Avoider is one that has some well-honed skill that helps them wriggle out of responsibility or blame. Often, they have unconsciously learned this skill over time and have put it to very good use, at times not even realizing that this is what they are doing, or at least highly unlikely to ever admit to it.

These skills could include exceptional language and logic skills, as they can talk their way out of anything due to their high intellect or exceptional vocabulary. Often, this ability is so good that they even convince themselves that they are right and that they were not responsible for something they clearly were. Essentially, they confuse or convince the other party of a new version of events or logic. They might create a sense of uncertainty in the person's belief as to what had happened or draw them into such a complex conversation that they simply relent. Gaslighting is a go-to for the Avoider.

Another skill set is charm or charisma. They not only have a way with words but also with their body language and facial expressions. They know all the right things to say and do, how to hold themselves, and just how much flirtation or flattery to use to get things over the line.

Perhaps you can remember a time when your partner managed to avert responsibility via a kiss or some flattery. Again, in mild cases, these strategies are often appropriate. It is when they are used disproportionately to the situation that one might start to consider it to be avoidance.

The Angry Avoider
This variant is perhaps a less sophisticated version of the skilled Avoider. Rather than learning how to effectively use humor or flattery, the Angry Avoider has learned to use fear and intimidation. Again, this is likely not due to some preference for anger, but rather it was possibly modeled to them, or they found it effective in earlier years, which led them to continue to unconsciously practice it and become skilled in it.

The Angry Avoider has learned that most people dislike conflict. By displaying displeasure or anger when first approached with the possibility of taking responsibility for an action, they escalate the conversation to signal, "This won't go well if you continue." They may become disproportionately emotional, animated, or loud. They may try to use some sort of deflection or logic as the "Skilled Avoider" does, but this is often secondary to their use of intimidation or anger.

This anger, as with any other skill set mentioned above, is a defensive structure relied upon to avert any suggestion that they are at fault. As mentioned earlier, this is done as the Avoider cannot tolerate the potential negative judgment that comes from being at fault. They have not learned that taking responsibility is a net gain for their development, as they are insecure within themselves.

Caution: We must be careful here not to misattribute where the anger has come from. Has it come as a direct result of the threat of them feeling blamed/held responsible? Or was it there prior to this due to some other cause?

Identification Considerations

Take careful note of *when* the Avoider is avoiding. It may well be that they only avoid responsibility at their workplace, or more commonly with their partner, or perhaps only in some specific area. This might signify that they are not an Avoider "globally," but rather only in the area where they lack security. For those who only avoid responsibility at work, they may be insecure about their professional ability. If they avoid taking responsibility with their spouse, then perhaps they lack emotional security and so on.

Whatever the case, generally speaking, if we can develop the levels of security in an Avoider or a Blamer, then we stand a chance of removing their need to rely on these approaches. However, it is important to keep in mind that these strategies are often deeply ingrained, and if nothing else, a lifelong habit, and they may take some time and effort to shift.

As with all the types explained so far, we need to look for long-term patterns of behavior. We should not be quick to label someone a Blamer or an Avoider due to one instance of doing so, or indeed one period of time doing so. We are all prone to blame or avoid at times. The question here is, has this person done so consistently across a wide range of situations and with a broad range of people? If someone is only ever avoiding responsibility with one person, we should analyze that relationship. Equally, if they only blame their family of origin but never blame their partner, children, friends, or co-workers, then again, we need to examine why this is.

Examples of this can be seen in their use of humor, affection, or other methods to deflect the issue. While these methods might be appropriate for minor issues, such as a broken glass, to lighten the mood and keep things in perspective, using them to minimize serious issues, like infidelity, clearly marks someone as an Avoider.

Should the Avoider be pushed beyond their deflecting and avoiding skills, they might take responsibility or resort to blame. Beneath the surface of an Avoider, there could be a Blamer or a Responsible person, but these are secondary, or backup used when their avoidant tactics fail.

How One Becomes an Avoider

The development of the Avoider is not too dissimilar to any of the childlike strategies in that its root lies in the lack of secure development throughout childhood and adolescence. The Avoider, much like the Blamer, never developed a sense of security in themselves, likely due to some deficits in their upbringing. Most commonly, this includes an absence of sufficient encouragement, love, and support as a child or as a result of direct aggression or trauma. Ultimately, a fundamental human need has not been fulfilled for them in their development, and they adapted to that lack by leaning towards a strategy that helped them survive at the time, i.e., blame their sibling or the dog or run and hide to avoid their mother's/father's wrath.

This may sound a lot like "parent blaming," but it is simply a matter of basic human development. There are countless studies and everyday observations of this dynamic playing out. It is not in debate that a child with a problematic household will be far more likely to do poorly at school, academically, socially, or behaviorally. Evidence of this can be garnered from any well-read psychologist, psychiatrist, experienced teacher, or childcare worker. It is a fundamental tenant of the human psyche that a person must first find safety and security. If this is provided, then we can move on to more advanced matters, but if it is not, then that insecurity and lack of self-belief is instilled into us and becomes part of the self (part of who we are).

The importance of receiving this safety and security from the home and the guardians of the child (parents primarily, but this could be others should parents not be present in the child's life) is paramount. This is not only because parents are the most likely individuals to love that child, but also because of the role-modeling nature they hold and the genetic similarity which often manifests in distinct similarity in traits between parent and child. Essentially, parents and children should be able to relate to each other to a greater extent due to the underlying traits they share due to their genetic makeup.

The Overly Responsible

In the above section, we looked at how self-blame works in this second layer of the Blame-Responsibility Dynamic. If we try to do the same with self-responsibility, we find that many of these variants are already explained in the Layer 1 understanding of this dynamic. This is likely due to the underlying principle that taking responsibility for oneself is an intrinsically adult and functional strategy, and so there are less complex or messy dynamics to unravel than in the case of the Self-blamer.

As we saw above, there are several ways in which self-blame can be problematic. However, in the case of responsibility, this changes. When a person takes responsibility for their actions, it reduces the number of ways things can become problematic. This is not to say things will go perfectly or without pain each time, but it certainly clears up the muddy waters of the "blame" approach. Simply speaking, taking responsibility seems to result in less problematic outcomes or at least fewer possible ways things could become problematic.

When it comes to responsibility takers, the only clear issue is when someone takes responsibility for things they are not responsible for. This can be problematic at times (or over time) but not always significantly so, or at least less problematic than other strategies.

Taking Responsibility for Others

This is the dynamic in which an individual takes responsibility for someone else when the responsibility is not theirs to take. This could be something as simple as a mother taking on the responsibilities of her children, an employee taking on the responsibilities of their boss or co-worker, a sibling taking responsibility for their younger (or perhaps older) siblings, and so on. In fact, there could be any number of relationships where this occurs. But is this problematic? And if so, how?

No matter how one looks at things, taking responsibility is always the more functional strategy compared to blame. However, there are *potential* issues with taking responsibility for something that is not genuinely yours. Earlier, when discussing the "Self-blamer," we mentioned the protective mother. This protective mother could be protecting her child from blame or responsibility. Further, she could be doing this by self-blaming or by being "Overly Responsible." The self-blaming mother will be negative towards herself, while the overly responsible will retain a degree of positivity or at least neutrality in her self-perception. So, where does this overly responsible strategy go wrong? For the mother, it can burden her with more and more "work," which can lead to being overworked and stressed and potentially falling into a state of anxiety or depression.

It is possible that this mother will start to grow resentment towards those she is willingly helping. This resentment is often unconscious. As she believes she is doing the right thing and being helpful by taking responsibility for others, she does not always grasp why she is also feeling anger towards these same people. Perhaps this later becomes obvious to her, and she starts to blame others for being "lazy" or "avoidant" of their responsibilities. Hence, we now have this Blame-Responsibility Dynamic playing out in a problematic way. The mother can hardly be blamed for feeling resentment, but she is responsible for allowing that resentment to grow within her. Perhaps ironically, her taking responsibility from others got in the way of her realizing she was not taking responsibility for herself.

The above example could just as easily play out in the workplace. An employee starts to take responsibility for their co-worker as they believe they are protecting their less capable co-worker from any fallout from management. They step in and do the work of the co-worker, and they come to feel this is their responsibility as the "better" worker or simply their duty as a "nice" person. Over time, they, too, get overworked and start to resent their co-worker for making their life difficult. Again, we can see how taking responsibility that is not our own can lead to problematic outcomes.

There is also the effect that this Overly Responsible strategy has on others. In the examples, the children and co-workers are both robbed of the opportunity to take responsibility for themselves and, therefore, robbed of the opportunity to learn, grow, and develop. If they are never given the opportunity to take responsibility, they will not learn the valuable lessons that come with it. They are also being encouraged not to take responsibility and run the risk of developing a sense of entitlement or laziness. In some cases, they may actually resent the Overly Responsible as they want to take the responsibility themselves.

Another possible risk for the Overly Responsible is that of being taken advantage of. There may be instances where others will recognize this tendency and use it to their advantage. The co-worker may realize they could benefit from such a person and do less, knowing the Over Responsible person will pick up the slack. This is also true for a mother and child. As loving as children might be, they are also very capable of getting what they can from a situation.

Keep it simple: The Overly Responsible can become stressed and resentful, as well as play a hand in others becoming lazy, entitled, or irresponsible.

How Does One Become Overly Responsible?

The reasons behind someone tending towards the Overly Responsible can vary. They might be conditioned to do so, like the Self-blamer, which is something you might see in an elder sibling or a child with incapable parents who constantly verge on self-destruction. There may be cases where a person correctly learns that responsibility leads to personal growth, but they over apply it and start taking responsibility from others, perhaps consciously with the belief it is good for them or unconsciously due to habit. There are other scenarios where someone may have a strong desire to control their environment (out of anxiety or a dominating nature), so they take on all the responsibility.

Each of the above possible reasons for developing an Overly Responsible strategy points towards environmental or social training factors, as they do with the Self-blame strategy. There may well also be a genetic component to this, but that is outside the scope of this book, and given the sheer volume of psychological theory and understanding around psychodynamics, it's safe to say there is plenty in the environment to warrant our attention in terms of understanding how this develops.

Overly Responsible Mindset
The mindset of the Overly Responsible is inherently positive, which is to say they believe they can cope with things as well as improve upon themselves. When they enact their over-responsibility, they are doing so with good intentions, be that to protect others or as an opportunity for continued self-growth. Their mindset, however, is one of "I am good enough, but I can always keep improving." While this is certainly a much healthier mindset than that of the Self-blamer, it is not without its flaws. Over time, it can lead to increasing stress and resentment, which can also lead to issues such as anxiety and depression. They also run the risk of preventing others from adequately developing their own sense of responsibility as the overly responsible unknowingly lift this responsibility from them.

Keep it simple: In the case of the Overly Responsible individual, there is no psychological injury other than the added burden of managing or resolving an issue for which they have taken responsibility. At best, it is another opportunity for them to rise to the occasion. The healthiness of taking on others' responsibilities depends greatly on their capacity to do so at the time, as any parent can attest. For example, bathing your child can result in a feeling of satisfaction and bonding on a good day, but it can seem insurmountable on a bad day.

The Takeaway

Ultimately, the Overly Responsible tend to be less prone to negative self-appraisal or at least have a less destructive mindset. Their tendency to take responsibility for others does not necessarily harm them, although it can if it is not managed or persists for too long. They also run the risk of preventing others from learning to take responsibility for themselves, which in turn robs them of their own learning and development.

The Narcissistic Partner

In the case of a narcissistic or sociopathic partner, the individual is often blamed for things that go wrong, as the narcissist will inherently be unable to take responsibility for themselves. After a time, the individual starts to learn that they will be blamed for anything that goes wrong. They identify that something has gone wrong and are conditioned to expect to be blamed.

At first, assuming they had self-esteem prior to the relationship, they will make attempts to defend themselves. However, should the relationship continue, they will come to learn they cannot win the argument with the narcissist (likely due to the narcissist's lifelong experience and expert level of manipulation). At this point, knowing that they will be blamed regardless of reality, they start to either believe the narcissist and therefore believe it was their fault (they have been successfully gaslit), or they simply learn to self-blame as this results in less emotional abuse from the narcissist.

In either case, prolonged exposure to this leads to a sense of helplessness by having been conditioned to blame themselves for everything. This behavior of taking the blame for their narcissistic partner can be globalized to every relationship they have. They have become convinced that they are constantly at fault and are conditioned to blame themselves at the first sign of a problem.

The Narcissistic Parent

The case of being conditioned by a narcissistic or sociopathic parent is much the same as that of a partner. However, it has an added layer of evil attached as it targets a helpless child who has not had the opportunity to know any better. This is the case of a parent who has never learned to take responsibility for themselves and blame their helpless child for their own shortcomings. The child has no defense, no prior learned ability to stand up for themselves, especially not against their "caregiver." The child will rely on their parents for survival, and now, in some sick twist, that same parent is conditioning the child to self-injure to alleviate themselves of any responsibility for wrongdoing.

Sadly, a child in such a position is likely to grow up believing they are a bad child and always do wrong or are at fault when something goes wrong. They will self-blame in advance of anyone taking responsibility because that is what their parent/s trained them to do. The child will always long to be accepted but will struggle to accept themselves, let alone be able to accept the acceptance of others, which they so desperately need.

In the case of being conditioned to self-blame at the hands of a romantic partner, the individual could have been very high functioning prior to their relationship. Over time, however, they have been manipulated into self-blaming for everything that may go wrong in that relationship and then, more widely, anything that goes wrong in either of their lives. In the case of a narcissistic and, therefore, manipulative parent/s, the person learns to self-blame from childhood, never having had a chance to develop any self-esteem or worth, leading them to lack assertiveness and struggle with any level of confrontation. Often, they will feel that they are less valuable than others, or at the very least, fear others, especially those who show any level of confidence (which can mimic the narcissism of their parent/s). PTSD is also a common outcome of such a childhood environment.

One can be impacted by any narcissist who has sufficient time and influence in our lives. This could extend to a boss, a sibling, a mentor, or even a culture or a government. In the end, this leads to a person who has either learned or been conditioned to doubt themselves. This situation benefits the narcissist, as the victim now relies on the narcissist for guidance or assistance. They become dependent on the narcissist as, over time, they have lost faith and trust in themselves. They defer to the "better" judgment of the narcissist as they have come to believe that they are the ones who have the answers, know best, or somehow actually care about them. Unfortunately, there is no shortage of individuals entering therapy as a result of a relationship with a narcissist. Along with having been conditioned to believe negatively of themselves, they often develop other issues such as depression, anxiety, a lack of self-identity, and general trauma.

What Influences Which Strategy We Take?

We have seen how the development of these mindsets is largely impacted by one's childhood, in that of how people were trained or conditioned by their parents and significant others. There may be genetic factors at play, such as those impacting one's temperament, intelligence, and any number of other possible factors. However, we cannot underestimate the impact of one's environment and how that environment impacts them. By environment, I am referring to their life experiences, as well as how those experiences were encoded and remembered.

Keep it simple: Which mindset we tend to adopt (blame, self-blame, responsibility, etc.) will depend on what we have experienced, how we have encoded that experience, and what message was

CHAPTER 4 – BLAME AND RESPONSIBILITY: THE NEXT LEVEL

given to us by our parents and significant others throughout our development.

This encoding and remembering is key to how a person understands their experience. How we encode our experiences will depend not just on what we *think* has happened in that experience but also on how others have influenced what we *think* has happened. We learn a lot about ourselves, the world, and its *rules* throughout our lives, particularly in early childhood (when we are most impressionable).

Take a simple example of a young child, perhaps three years old, who breaks a toy or household item. Their first instinct will likely be to look at their nearest parent. They do this to learn how to respond. They know something has just been broken, so they check with their parent to see if they are in trouble or not, if they should cry at the loss of the item or laugh at its expectancy. How their parent responds in that instant will very much impact how that child encodes that experience. The look on the parent's face is enough to influence this, and what they say or do in response will further entrench the child's encoding. If the parent shows anger and yells "Bad boy!" at the child, then they are likely to encode this negatively and put a metaphorical token in the "negative mindset" jar. If the parent shows joyful surprise followed by some kind or supportive words like, "Wow, look how strong you are! Now you have two smaller toys!" then the child is more likely to encode this positively, or at least not negatively, which pushes them more towards a positive mindset. This same principle plays out dozens, if not hundreds, of times a day in early life, quickly adding up to the development of a child's mindset.

Keep it simple: None of us choose our childhood; we are all victims of it. Therefore, which strategy we adopt is very much based on elements outside of our control. People tend not to choose an unhelpful strategy for life, so if they have one, they may not be aware of it and are unlikely to have chosen it willingly.

Blame and Responsibility in "Positive" Scenarios

We have only looked at scenarios where something negative has occurred, such as a child breaking a window, but this dynamic, or its underlying principles of secure development, holds true in instances of positive outcomes, too. Consider the scenario where someone scores 99% on an exam. This would generally be considered a positive outcome. However, rather than taking responsibility for their hard work and subsequent good grades, they blame themselves for not scoring 100%. Or perhaps they give credit or responsibility for that good grade to their tutor and insist that they would have failed without that tutor's help.

There are other psychological factors at play in the above scenario, and in truth, the Blame-Responsibility Dynamic may not be the best explanatory model for this, but it can certainly be viewed from this lens. In cases like this, the person's inability to take responsibility (or credit) for their achievements is often once again tied to their esteem or their self-belief. There are plenty of people willing to swoop in and take credit from others, which may reinforce the individual's reluctance to take on this "positive" responsibility—or, ideally, provoke them enough to begin doing so.

Here's a recap of some of the important things to keep in mind before determining someone to be any of the types discussed:

- There needs to be a consistent pattern of behavior. We should not label someone as a Blamer, an Avoider, Responsible, or otherwise unless we see this consistent pattern.
- Context is important. Their pattern of behavior may be tied to a particular person or place, be that a partner, a child, a boss, a workplace, a home, or when on vacation.
- Some types share traits. The Blamer and the Avoider are both irresponsible and may have similar approaches to an issue. For example, both could use anger to achieve their goal of not taking responsibility.
- A person can be more than one type. It is possible that a person has layers of these strategies. For example, the Avoider may use

avoidance as their primary method, but when that fails, they become a Blamer. Equally, the Responsible individual may also be prone to being Overly Responsible or even self-blaming at times, depending on the context of the situation.

The Takeaway

When reviewing the factors at play in the blaming versus responsibility strategies, there is a theme of negativity versus positivity. (Keep in mind that these mindsets are developed and not chosen.) In many ways, this could also be viewed as anxiety or low esteem versus confidence or high esteem, as negativity and anxiety tend to go together, whereas confidence and positivity also tend to travel in close circles.

When looking at the variations of this Blame-Responsibility in layers 2 and 3, there are more nuances as to why a person might develop as a, say, Self-blamer rather than Overly Responsible. Nuances such as their conditioning or encoding of experiences, the influence of role models, whether their parents instilled confidence, which led to a path of taking responsibility, whether they learned blame from a parent, or if they experienced childhood abuse. There are any number of possible factors, and it is how a person interrupts the experience as much as it is the experience itself. After all, it is how we understand and remember something that impacts us more than any experience itself. In our younger years, this processing and understanding can be difficult, as our brains are still very underdeveloped. Perhaps for this reason, good parental guidance is key.

The difference between the Overly Responsible and the Self-blamer is primarily that of their mindset, positive versus negative, respectively. The direction in which this mindset develops is largely dependent on the messages that accompany the experiences that we have throughout our development. That is to say, the messaging we receive from those around us influences how we encode or remember that experience. If those around us are supportive, kind, and helpful, then we are more likely to encode things positively. However, if they are more negative, blaming, and attacking, we are more likely to form a negative mindset.

Of course, there are genetic factors that play a role here, such as temperament, intelligence, and likely a host of others. However, these are not factors we can control, and so I argue that our best approach to positive change is to focus on the area we can control— the messages or influences we place on others and, in particular, children.

We have mentioned how a person can develop or evolve based on which strategy of blame or responsibility they take. Ultimately, there are more unhelpful strategies than helpful ones. We see that blaming others is an avoidant strategy that prevents personal growth while burdening or damaging others. Blaming yourself is self-destructive as it not only prevents your emotional growth but actively destroys self-esteem and self-acceptance. Being overly responsible, that is, taking responsibility from others, prevents them from their own growth while burdening or over-inflating yourself. The healthiest way to develop personally and emotionally is by responsibly and thoughtfully taking ownership of oneself.

Keep it simple: For those looking to correct their life path towards a healthy, harmonious one, both with themselves and with others, you must become aware of your mindset and then choose to actively change it. Identify which strategy of blame and responsibility you have developed, then actively work on correcting it. Always remember that the only approach that yields healthy adult development is that of personal responsibility.

While having the ability to take responsibility and take suitable actions to address any shortcomings is in essence the difference between an emotionally developed adult and a child (even if that child is well into their 40s or 50s), one does not suddenly become 'adult' just by starting to take responsibility. The emotional development comes from the process of taking responsibility over time. It is the lessons learned from taking responsibility in each given situation that starts to shape ones character and therefore develop them into an adult.

For example a 40 year old man who has behaved like a child his whole life cannot simply tell his wife one day that he is taking responsibility for something, and therefore that makes him a mature and emotionally developed man. Taking out the trash for the first time, doesn't instantly make you a responsible and reliable grown up, especially if it was only done to obtain some sense of status or approval. Should this man consistently take out the trash, without fail, and then find himself taking on other chores unprompted, then he has started to develop some degree of maturity and responsibility.

Keep it simple: Its the consequence of taking responsibility that creates the adult, not the responsibility directly.

When taking responsibility over a long period of time, and in a broad context, we start to be faced with our true nature, our characteristics, values and emotions. We are then faced with the choice of whether or not we are going to work on these factors, or simply maintain the status quo (not develop). In the case of 'children', regardless of their age, they fail to make this choice, they are often not aware there was a choice to be made as they have little or no insight to the impacts of their actions. Or perhaps they choose to ignore those impacts. This often looks like selfishness to others, and it is this selfishness that blinds the person to the fact that there is a choice to examine ones actions, and perhaps change them.

Throughout the process of taking responsibility we are faced by many human values or traits, which gives us the opportunity to develop them should we make the effort to do so. So what are some of these traits that come from responsibility?

Resilience is certainly one of them. No one can consistently take responsibility for their actions and address them without it teaching them resilience. Being faced with the reality that you have repeatedly made mistakes, or even failed, only to then take it upon yourself to find a way to address the issue and make it right, will tend to teach a person that they can, and will, continue to get up after being knocked down.

Humility is another, having to acknowledge your mistakes directly, and repeatedly, will no doubt keep a person in check; its hard not to be humble when you have daily reminders of how prone you are to slipping up in one way or another. This equally helps to prevent someone from becoming arrogant, after all if you are aware of just how human and imperfect you are, then it can be difficult to maintain your arrogance.

This humility and awareness of arrogance in turn starts to develop other traits, such as compassion and understanding. By this stage in the process of responsibility you are not only aware of how easy it is to fall short on something, you are also well aware of how unpleasant it is to face that feeling. You will have countless experience of not being proud of yourself, especially the times when others where there to see or hear it. Knowing how uncomfortable that feeling is, how much you wanted to run away from it, and how tempting it was to blame someone else rather than wear that guilt or shame, is what teaches you that others are going through the same thing. When someone else lies, or blames, it is likely because they are unable to tolerate the unpleasant feeling that you know all too well. Your struggles with responsibility have given you insight to others actions, which has made you more understanding, and should you choose, more compassionate.

Knowing what they are facing rather than just how they are acting gives you the opportunity to choose your words wisely, show that compassion, and very likely start to help them deal with the difficult emotions they are facing. At this point, this process of taking responsibility has also made you wiser, more helpful, and likely more likable if not more valuable.

With this growth in compassion and empathy, you realize we are more alike than we are different, and that despite our differences, we largely function on similar internal structures or personal battles. With some luck, or effort, this new found understanding of commonality with others can come to make you realize that although you are unique, you are no different to others, and therefore you deserve no more or less than they do.

All of these traits, or characteristics then tend to combine over time, you become more self aware, you also become more assured of your ability to manage yourself within the world. After all, having taken responsibility for decades tends to teach you what your limits are as a person, along with the realization that you can resolve a lot more of life's issues that you once thought. This of course tends to make a person more confident, which in turn reduces their anxiety; and so the cycle goes.

Keep it simple: Over time, taking responsibility creates a capable person who knows their limits, who has greater control over themselves and therefore their lives.

Chapter 5 – Addressing Responsibility

There are a number of ways and opportunities for a person to develop a greater sense of responsibility. Ideally, this starts in childhood, with attentive parents who ensure the child's safety and security, which, in this case, is emotional safety and security. They take the time to support and guide the child during times of emotional struggle and learning and encourage them to take on age-appropriate levels of responsibility over time. Keep in mind that any child will only learn what they are shown or exposed to. No child spontaneously learns to speak or understand a second language that they have never heard, nor are they likely to spontaneously learn how to be responsible if they have never been taught or exposed to it. The same can be said for any emotionally challenging scenario that a child faces, but that is perhaps beyond the scope of the current topic.

How to Build Responsibility

For those not so fortunate to have parents who took the time or indeed realized the need for such guidance and support, the question remains: how does an adult (or adolescent) develop their ability to take responsibility? One could enter into psychotherapy, which, if done with a skilled therapist, can be very beneficial as it grows one's knowledge of themselves. If that is not an option, or one is not yet ready for such a step, they could consider the below steps as a starting point:

1. Be aware of the impacts of your actions (on self and others).
2. Take on change as a positive challenge, not a negative reflection of self.

3. Speak to and encourage yourself as you would a loved one (friend, partner, child).
4. Focus on who you want to (and will) become rather than who you believe you currently are.
5. Avoid the trappings of blame, both from yourself and others.

Being Aware of the Impacts of Your Actions

One of the common features of irresponsible people is that they're not aware of how their actions impact others, or they're not adequately motivated to take responsibility. There is a third grouping of people who simply do not care how they impact others. These individuals typically fit into the narcissist and sociopath group, which we won't explore here.

Most adults are responsible to a certain degree, or at least about specific things. This is because they are often aware of the need to be responsible in those areas, knowing the consequences of not being responsible.

For example, someone may be responsible with their job and turn up each day, know what is required of them and get the job done consistently. They know these things are required in order to maintain their job and, therefore, income. Some might even take pride in their identity as a good worker or simply do not want to burden others by being lazy in their work. Ultimately, this person is a responsible worker. However, when they get home, they fail to take responsibility for their chores, don't take out the bins, laze about and argue when confronted about this lack of responsibility. They are not responsible in their domestic life in the way they are in their professional life. This stark contrast between a person's work and home responsibility levels could be because:

- They don't take pride in their role as a partner/parent/family member as they do with their job/profession. This could be an indication that they have more respect for their coworkers than they do for their family, or they value their identity as a good worker more than they do their identity as a good family member.

- They only take responsibility at work to get a reward (an income) and they do not see a reward being offered in the home. This particular attitude might suggest a selfish or short-sighted nature.
- They do not realize the negative impact their inaction has on those at home and they do not perceive any negative impact, so they assume the behavior is appropriate or at least acceptable in that environment. At work, they may well get fired, sent home, and have their pay docked. But at home, there are few, if any, negative consequences, and so they learn that they can simply get away with being irresponsible. They are being taught to be irresponsible.

So, they are either unaware of the impact of their actions or aware that there is not a significant enough consequence for being irresponsible at home to make them change (no adequate motivator). This difference does not necessarily have to be between work and home; it could be across any environment, between certain friendships, or in any sphere of life.

Keep it simple: To improve one's ability to take responsibility, we must first be consciously aware of how avoiding responsibility impacts us and others.

Actions, Outcomes, Awareness, Improvement

Throughout my clinical practice, one of the things I have found is that a person first needs to realize how their choices impact outcomes. Unless you know the impacts of your actions, you have little to guide the correction or continuation of that action.

This plays out on both obvious and subtle levels. An obvious example might be someone realizing that they play a key role in a team. If they take responsibility for themselves and do their best, then the team is more likely to do well. Equally, if they fail to turn up or make no effort, then the team is more likely to do poorly. The individual's choice to try their best or not directly affects the team's outcome, indicating that they hold a degree of responsibility for the team's success or failure. In this example, it may become quite obvious for the individual how their choices impact the team's performance if they bother to examine it or if it is pointed out by their coach/manager. As long as they see the impacts of their actions, they can be guided by it, should they choose to do so. If trying leads to better results for the team, then they can be aware of this and act accordingly.

If the team does well, regardless of whether this person is trying or not, then the person has no sense of agency or influence within the team. They cannot determine if they are helping the team. Without feedback, they do not know which course of action is best to take. Their actions seem to have no impact, leading them to question whether they should make an effort or not.

The more subtle version of this example is when the team does only slightly better or worse depending on the individual's efforts. It may well be possible that the team does well all the time, regardless of the individual's decision to make an effort or not. The team might be just that good, or perhaps the other team members are working harder to compensate for the individual choosing to put in less effort. If all we did was look at the overall outcome, the individual might start to think that their level of effort, low as it may be, is all that is required, and therefore there is no issue. This is the point where they choose not to take responsibility for their actions because it is difficult to know with certainty what impact their actions have.

If one does not realize how their actions impact the world around them, it is easier to minimize or ignore the impacts of their actions and continue. Even if it is clear to others that these actions are having a negative impact, if the person themselves does not see or understand the impact of their action, they have little incentive to change them. In fact, if they do not have awareness, then they might understandably argue or disagree with those who point out flaws or issues with these actions. From their point of view, they are doing nothing wrong and will defend themselves simply because they do not "see" the impact of their actions. Equally, they may fail to see the positives of their own actions and fail to give themselves credit or believe others when they give them praise for their actions. This latter scenario is often seen in those with low self-esteem, anxiety, or depression.

As a visual example of this, consider a 3-year-old who innocently throws a toy at a wall and smiles gleefully. As far as they are concerned, they just did something amazing: they made the toy fly! They have no idea that their actions resulted in damage to the toy and the wall, which may now be a financial expense to someone. The child certainly did not intend to cause financial loss; they are oblivious to such things. Similarly, some adults are oblivious to the actual outcomes of their actions, often by choice or ignorance rather than cognitive limitations, as was the case with the child.

Keep it simple: Accurately understanding the outcomes of your actions is an important factor in developing the understanding of why we should be responsible, as well as a step in starting to take responsibility.

Building one's ability to realize how they impact things can bring awareness to what they are and are not responsible for. At times, building this awareness can lead them to realize they are avoiding a problem or blaming someone or something else for their problem. Once they realize this, they gain a sense of power over their problem and their environment. They also assume responsibility for themselves, stepping into adulthood, at least for the moment.

Sometimes, this "moment" of understanding is enough of an epiphany that it constitutes change for a lifetime. Other times, it is enough for a short-term change, and sadly, sometimes, it is only enough for a moment of clarity, which makes them feel improved with no change in their future actions. The first option results in an almost instant resolution of the issue, although this is a rare occasion.

CHAPTER 5 – ADDRESSING RESPONSIBILITY

The second is the short-term impact, which can be built upon. If the individual has enough of these "moments," then the short-term changes can start to string together and create a new habit of behavior. In any case, awareness or understanding will precede any active change in the person.

Consider this in the scenario of an adult male who is constantly causing drama or injury of some sort. Perhaps he is repeatedly neglecting his partner. This partner becomes upset and eventually reacts to it. However, this male has gone months, if not years, of neglecting behavior with no concept of its impact on his partner or their relationship. The partner may or may not have mentioned it repeatedly, but in any case, it never sunk into the male's awareness. He never clearly linked his behavior with an outcome. At least not until the partner had packed their bags and left.

Often, things such as this are due to a person choosing to avoid an issue or simply not recognizing the extent of the issue. Once they have realized it, or they choose to stop avoiding it, they are able to instigate some change. In either case, they are now aware that the responsibility for what happens next is entirely theirs. They can no longer blame others or blame circumstances for their current situation—it is their choice that is perpetuating their circumstance. This is not to say that they are the root cause of the issue, but they are certainly responsible for perpetuating it if they are failing to take responsibility for their contribution.

As an example, take a person who has had a loved one pass away. It's likely they are not responsible for the death of their loved one, and they have every reason to be sad, angry, depressed, or otherwise grieving the loss. They now have a decision to make about how they manage this situation. They can attempt to ignore the feelings and act as though nothing has changed; they can allow their feelings to overcome them and act out, or they can choose to take responsibility for their actions despite their feelings. What they choose and when will determine their experience of that loss. It is important to note here that these choices are often not active ones, and in many cases, people do not actively think about such things but simply allow their unconscious to decide their choices for them.

Someone who decides to process the loss might choose to take some time off work, spend time with family and friends who knew the person, reflect on the value of the person who has passed away, attend some form of ritual, such as a funeral, burial, or vigil to help process the loss, and then gradually reengage with their life. Whereas someone opting not to deal with the loss might do nothing different to what they did prior to the loss, or they may "numb" their feelings via self-medicating. They may embrace their anger or sadness and isolate themselves. They may even blame the deceased rather than take responsibility for their own feelings. Ultimately, the deceased is not responsible for the individual's feelings or life direction, that rests in the hands of the individual. The question is whether or not they realize this and at what point.

Keep it simple: Make a person realize how their choices/actions/thoughts impact their world, and they will become aware of their responsibility. Whether they choose to take that responsibility remains their choice. Equally, have a person realize their lack of responsibility is creating issues in their life, and they become empowered to decide if they want to address this or not.

Often, the awareness of how one's actions contribute to their life problems is enough to motivate change. They realize they have the power to positively affect their own lives (or the lives of those around them), so they take that opportunity to make positive changes. This whole process is in the aid of developing understanding or insight in the person. They need to realize that they should take responsibility for their actions or thoughts, and then they can start to exercise greater control over their lives.

Rewarded Irresponsibility

The above section is largely directed toward individuals interested in personal growth through taking responsibility for their actions. However, this is not always the case. Some people are fully aware of their actions but continue to choose to avoid responsibility because it serves their interests. This behavior can occur not only in individuals but also in groups, organizations, and cultures.

The sad reality of human nature is that in its breadth, there are those who have absolutely no intention of taking responsibility, ownership, or even admission of their actions. As far as I have noticed, they do this for two reasons:

1) it is profitable for them not to, and
2) there are no repercussions for not taking responsibility.

Take the arrogant, powerful owner of a manufacturing company. They process some natural resources and produce a toxic byproduct as part of that process. Rather than disposing of these toxic products safely, which is costly, they dump them into a local river (a not uncommon reality). If there are negative consequences for such behavior, the company may refrain from repeating it in the future, irrespective of whether they took responsibility for the act initially. However, if there is no or insufficient consequence, they have no reason to take responsibility or change their actions. They learn that avoiding responsibility for their actions is profitable and has no negative consequences. When given the chance to avoid responsibility, such companies or individuals will naturally take it. It's inherent to their nature and expecting them to behave otherwise would be unreasonable. In fact, one could argue that we are at fault for expecting them to behave otherwise, we are applying our moral beliefs onto them, and expecting they should comply (this is further explored in the following chapter). In the case of this irresponsible company, the only solution for positive change or behavior improvement is for others to hold the company responsible and to do so in no uncertain or no mitigated terms. This concept is further explored in Factor 2: The Primary Pitfall.

In this example, we could just as well identify those who are tasked with regulating such behavior as irresponsible, for they permit and encourage the behavior by failing to enforce adequate consequences for the company or individual. On a broader level, it is the full range of human nature that is required to keep it in check. If the "good" does not hold the "bad" to account, then the bad perpetuates. One might even question the existence of good if it is not combating the bad.

The above example equally translates to an individual. Consider a shoplifter. If they are caught and not punished or punished with insufficient consequences, what reason do they have to change their behavior? Equally, can we blame a child for avoiding responsibility if we have taught them how to avoid it? I would argue the parent would be to blame for the child's action, much as a governing body could be to blame for a company's deception as they not enforced sufficient ramifications at earlier stages of development.

Keep it simple: Some learn to actively avoid taking responsibility because it is profitable, especially in an environment where there are no repercussions for bad behavior.

The example of the polluting company above is simply a case of learned behavior. People learn that taking responsibility is less beneficial than avoiding responsibility simply because that is what the environment or society permits. It may be the case that these people are despised by some (or perhaps most), but the reality is the accumulative profit they find outweighs any negative opinions they might receive, not to mention their likely complete lack of care about what opinions the masses hold of them.

People generally act in a way that benefits themselves, and some people have learned that immoral action is rewarding. Further, they place no value in "developing their sense of responsibility." Instead, they value profit (monetary or otherwise) and hide behind something, such as the company, in an attempt to distance themselves from any immoral or questionable actions. Real-life examples of this are nearly endless. Consider any company or person that was found to be causing harm for profit. How many were required to give up all their gains and repay an equal amount in damages and/or serve a prison sentence versus those who were permitted to resign, take a company bonus, then work in a similar role and retire in luxury?

Keep it simple: Choosing not to take responsibility can be a personally beneficial stance, albeit at the expense of others. If a person or group embraces personal gain over responsibility, then it falls to others to hold them accountable should they desire a change in their actions.

To bring this example back to a more typical scenario, consider an employer paying people below minimum wage while they themselves live in excess, all while not being held to account. Or perhaps a young child is permitted to break the rules by parents who are inadvertently teaching them to push boundaries and see what they can get away with. The scale of impact is drastically different, but the underlying dynamic and learning are the same.

How to Take Responsibility for Yourself

Perhaps more difficult is that of learning to take responsibility when one has done something that is harmful or otherwise causes a degree of shame or regret. Often, it is difficult to admit fault or take responsibility when we feel a negative emotion. So, how does one learn to take responsibility in such a situation?

The difficulty that one faces here is that of overcoming any inner fears of being shamed or disproved of for their action. This could come from others or from within themselves. The defining factor here that will determine if they can take responsibility in such cases is whether or not they have the emotional strength to bear the burden of feeling disapproved of or otherwise negatively impacted. Often, there are thoughts that any guilt, shame, or disapproval that may result will remain *forever!* In reality, this is, of course, rarely the case and is often understood by the person themselves once questioned. However, even the momentary disapproval or shame is beyond what they *believe* they can tolerate. Therefore, they are more likely to want to avoid any responsibility that could lead to such an outcome.

So, how can you remedy this? How does a person come to a stage of development where they can tolerate this negative appraisal? There are many paths, but at the core, there is always a sense of safety or certainty that they will survive, even if there is a form of injury as a result. It all comes back to that young child trying to ensure its survival.

A person who has a great deal of self-esteem or self-belief and is confident in their ability to emotionally recover (or not be injured) from any disapproval or loss will have little difficulty taking responsibility. These are the individuals who have likely had a supportive upbringing, perhaps good friends and family or are otherwise capable in some way. They trust in their likability and emotional resilience or in their competence and ability to recover financially, such as in situations where taking responsibility might impact their employment. Interestingly, there is also a type of person that takes on the responsibility without the self-confidence described above, that being the person who holds some religious belief that they are looked after or saved regardless. These people find their safety and security not in people or themselves but in a higher being, such as God—they feel safe taking responsibility as they trust they are accepted and will be safe regardless.

However, those without these safeguards are far more emotionally fragile; their self-belief or security has not had a chance to develop. They likely constantly live on the precipice of fearing rejection or at least "nonacceptance," so taking responsibility is a dangerous prospect, and they are far more emotionally fragile than others. They are the emotional equivalent of a 90-year-old with osteoporosis taking the field at the

CHAPTER 5 – ADDRESSING RESPONSIBILITY

Superbowl and being expected to perform like everyone else on. Unlike this 90-year-old with osteoporosis, one can develop the emotional strength to take responsibility. However, it does take significant effort and support to achieve this. These individuals are more likely to tend towards self-blame. As discussed in previous chapters, this issue needs to be addressed by building their sense of self-worth, which is likely underdeveloped. Essentially, the core focus should be on improving one's self-belief and sense of safety. It's crucial to create an environment or instill a belief that they will be safe and will survive if they take responsibility. Over time, as they practice this, they come to realize that they are becoming more capable and that it's rare for the threats they envisioned from taking responsibility to materialize.

Keep it simple: We take responsibility when we believe we can survive any possible negative outcomes. Confidence in survival leads to a greater propensity to take responsibility, which leads to greater growth due to having taken responsibility.

Since people are a complex assortment of their experiences, there are, of course, other factors that contribute to their ability to take responsibility. However, one of the strong themes is this sense of security in oneself and the belief that one can tolerate any potential negative impacts of taking responsibility. If they have sufficient security, then they can tolerate the emotional difficulty of taking responsibility and, as such, have a greater opportunity to grow within themselves.

Often, our fears are greater than the reality of what comes to pass. Our minds exaggerate how bad things can be rather than accurately determine how bad things are likely to be, a trait shared by anyone with an anxiety disorder. In many cases, people are forgiving and tend not to react as negatively as we fear they might. Essentially, this means if we learn to be more accurate in our appraisal of others' "disapproval", we may find more courage to take responsibility.

Keep it simple: Often, those who fear responsibility lack emotional safety or security. This is usually a product of their upbringing rather than something innately within them. This can be improved by building a sense of safety and acceptance by those around them.

Perhaps the greatest way to improve your ability to take responsibility is to simply start doing so with small, everyday opportunities. Start with minor things. For example, if you ate one too many chocolate biscuits and find yourself blaming yourself, you might think, "Oh, I'm so bad. I had too many of these. I've totally blown my diet again. I'm so bad at diets, I can't even get that right!" This thought, or self-talk, can be easily shifted to one of responsibility as we move from a negative self-review to one that is far more helpful and less damaging: "Yeah, I just ate too many of these. I didn't need it, but I was feeling weak. Maybe I didn't get enough positivity in my day, so I ended up eating more to feel better. Tomorrow, I'll do things differently." This self-talk acknowledges your disappointment about eating too much, but it adds some self-compassion. It sets a mindset of improving rather than disapproving. You might also think, "I have to find some more positive feelings tomorrow to reduce my unconscious desire to eat to feel better. Maybe I'll call my friend Bob, he's always nice. And if I can't get through to him, I'll go for a run or take a relaxing bath." This follow-up self-talk creates achievable ideas and goals for the next day. If nothing else, this can help one feel good about their positive efforts to help themselves.

At this point, the individual has taken responsibility for their actions and created a plan to do better tomorrow. Even if their plan fails, they have had a positive, supportive, and encouraging discussion with themselves. If they find themselves grabbing one too many biscuits the next day, their brain will be more aware of what they are about to do. They have a greater chance of remembering their self-talk and pausing before putting that biscuit in their mouth. This pause provides a moment of time to reflect on how they want to feel: do they continue with the biscuit and feel rewarded now, or do they delay this in favor of feeling good about their choice to take responsibility and refrain? It can be that singular moment in time that turns the tide in both behavior and starting to build esteem by taking responsibility. On the other hand, if they stuck with the blaming voice, the one that was harsh towards them, then they have little incentive not to eat the biscuit. They are already expecting negative self-appraisal, so they may as well feel good for the few seconds that it takes to finish that biscuit before they fall back into self-loathing and irresponsibility.

Other ideas might include taking responsibility for not vacuuming your home, being late to an event, or dropping a fork, not because these things make a significant difference in themselves but because they will help you realize you can tolerate the responsibility and that taking responsibility is not life-ending.

Recall the young child who fears that responsibility leads to abandonment and death. That child still exists within an adult who cannot take responsibility. What we are really doing here is teaching that inner child that taking responsibility does not result in abandonment and death. If we can start with small tasks, we are slowly teaching that inner child age-appropriate ways to learn that responsibility can be a safe and beneficial strategy in life. At the very least, you start to become more comfortable and skilled with the self-talk you use. You learn it's not so bad, and you discover that you have far more authority over your day and yourself. With this comes the knowledge of your abilities and the growth of your confidence. This process can then extend to more significant matters, such as making a mistake at work, neglecting to consider your partner's feelings, etc.

Keep it simple: Should one take the time to make the effort, responsibility can lead to growth and improved outcomes.

The Gains of Taking Responsibility

The ways in which one can practice taking responsibility for one's actions and, indeed, one's life are limited only by how active one is in life. Perhaps, then, it's a matter of taking responsibility for one's inaction. The more opportunity you have to take responsibility for yourself, the more you learn about yourself. Initially, it shows us the way in which we are perhaps under performing, and it is reasonable to suggest that, at first, it is a humbling, if not unpleasant, experience.

No one wants to be made painfully aware of their shortcomings, but by doing so without negative judgment, we quickly become aware of what we can improve. We learn what our current and real ability is rather than permit ourselves to live in the pseudo-fantasy of who we think we are and what we think we are capable of. We all hold this disparity between who we think we are and who we actually are. Some think they are "better" than they are, while others think they are "less" than what they really are. The latter is something I have witnessed consistently with those suffering with anxiety. Sadly, some of the nicest people I have met are clients who unfairly hold negative opinions of themselves. Despite possessing amazing traits such as kindness, compassion, generosity, and intelligence, they are convinced they are unworthy, selfish, or stupid. This inner conflict is a cruel manifestation of a good person with a poor or undernourished upbringing. In any case, starting this process of taking responsibility will quickly start to bring your real self to the fore, and from there, we can start to improve upon it.

Keep it simple: Taking responsibility will initially require a degree of emotional tolerance and humility. It will also give you a greater and more accurate understanding of yourself and start the process of self-improvement.

As you continue this process of identifying and taking responsibility for yourself, your understanding of yourself improves.

CHAPTER 5 – ADDRESSING RESPONSIBILITY

You will start to improve in the areas that you have taken responsibility for, and ultimately, you learn your true capacity and limitations. This means you start to have a more accurate understanding of your actual self and far more control over what skills you choose to improve in. Beyond this, it also means that you will have a much greater ability to predict actual outcomes that involve your input. Once you know your capability, you know what you can accurately expect of yourself. This not only gives you a greater sense of security around what is to come, but when outcomes align with expectations, we tend to be happier in general. As hard as the path of taking responsibility may be at times, it results in:

- greater personal growth or development
- less negative self-talk and more self-esteem
- improved accuracy of understanding your abilities and limits
- better prediction of your outcomes
- increased security
- generally increased levels of happiness.

And all of this for the low, low price of some personal discomfort as you learn to tolerate some "potential" criticism or disapproval.

An Example of Responsibility Leading to Emotional Growth

Take someone who is emotionally insensitive to others. They can inadvertently say or do things that are harmful to others. Should they "choose" to take on feedback from others, or at least be aware of how others respond to them, then they can start to choose to take responsibility for the words they use with others. Choosing to accept responsibility for the "part" that they played can lead to them learning to become more careful in the future and more sensitive to others. Ultimately, they are becoming more emotionally capable and aware.

This is not to say they will never inadvertently upset anyone, but it will improve their ability to identify what might upset someone. Of note, I say their "part" in causing the upset, as the other party may well have contributed to their own distress. It is quite possible that they overvalued the person's words, personalized something they should not have, or otherwise failed to take responsibility for their own part in the exchange. Despite this, as long as one takes responsibility for their part, rather than dismissing it as the other person overreacting (even if they had), then the person stands to learn from the exchange, and should they make an effort, they can learn to become more sensitive or supportive in future exchanges.

Continuing from the above example, once a person has learned to take responsibility and acted on this by considering how to do better in the future, they should also take the time to consolidate a new understanding of themselves. When they start to apply this new learning repeatedly and mostly successfully, they should start to form a new and better understanding of who they are. They have transformed from being insensitive to becoming more sensitive. Now, they should have greater self-belief that they are no longer the type of person who unknowingly upsets others. Their journey has seen them evolve from insensitivity to sensitivity. They can be confident in their ability to be supportive of others when needed and confident that they are unlikely to inadvertently cause emotional distress to others. This process is further explored in Factor 4: The Take-home Message.

It's also true, albeit a darker aspect, that they should now be more aware of what does and doesn't cause distress to others. If they so choose, they could equally opt to cause distress to others. While many consider this morally unacceptable, the objective reality is that this ability is also a skill. It develops through taking the time to take responsibility for oneself and learning from one's experiences. Should this same person choose to cause distress or not, they have become a more capable person. The application and morality of this "capability" is another matter. Distasteful as it may be, a psychologist is trained in how the mind works. They typically use this knowledge to help others, but this same knowledge is also used to fuel marketing campaigns directed at parting people with their money. Both applications are effective, and you can decide which is the more ethical use of that knowledge.

The above example references the area of emotional responsibility and growth, but the same can be said for other areas, such as physical health, intellectual pursuits, or any areas in life that one is trying to improve upon. Taking responsibility for your failures at work can lead to getting more training, paying more attention, trying harder, and, ultimately, improving your skill sets in that department. It's important to note that taking responsibility in itself does not improve a person; it is the effort put in afterward that brings about change. Taking responsibility for being bad at your job won't improve your work performance; it's the subsequent effort you put into addressing the issue that makes the change. Once this effort is made, one stands to improve their ability in any given area and can critically appraise it by continuing to take responsibility. Over time, this leads to a realistic appraisal of one's new and improved ability, and as such, one has an awareness of their ability or limits. This brings confidence in their ability and, importantly, gives them a more accurate understanding of what outcomes to expect. This is a vital stage in overall development, as the more accurately we can predict an outcome, the lower our levels of anxiety are. This, in turn, leads to improved performance and mental health.

Keep it simple: The key to growth and better outcomes is taking responsibility, putting in effort to improve, understanding our abilities and limits, and gaining confidence in achieving our goals. This leads to less anxiety, more security via greater sense of outcome, and the ability to set realistic expectations, resulting in greater happiness and less disappointment.

What Causes Us to Become Responsible?

Why is it that some people can stick to this path of learning to take responsibility while others shy away from it? And what can we do to keep someone on this path long enough to make the transformation? Broadly speaking, the answer to this perhaps lies in the field of psychology called "behavioralism," a field of psychology that explores the nature of behaviors as a whole. If we were to shortcut this to a more immediate answer, I would suggest that the answer be motivation.

The field of behavioralism speaks about how people, and animals in general, learn to behave as they do. One of the principles of behavioralism is that of motivation via positive and negative reinforcement. Essentially, this theory states that we learn to repeat certain behaviors by receiving a reward for that behavior (positive reinforcement), or we learn to avoid a behavior by being punished for that behavior (negative reinforcement). A typical example of positive reinforcement would be a dog will learn to sit if it is given a reward for doing so, such as a treat, being scratched behind the ear, or having its ball thrown for them. A typical example of negative reinforcement would be a dog learns not to pee in the house when it is punished for doing so, such as having its nose rubbed in the pee or being yelled at/interrupted while in the act of peeing.

As long the dog can link their behavior with the reward or punishment that was given, then they can learn to either repeat or avoid that behavior in the future. People are no different from animals in this regard. If a person can learn that doing a good job at work gets them a bonus or a promotion, they are more likely to do that behavior. Equally, if they realize that not helping around the house leads to arguments or some other significant punishment, they are less likely to repeat that behavior (again, this is assuming this punishment is significant enough, as explored earlier).

Note: Regarding motivation, there are many people in the world of psychology who suggest that negative reinforcement is less effective than positive reinforcement. There is, however, also evidence for the effectiveness of "flooding," which is often viewed as a negative experience initially. In any case, negative reinforcement is largely discouraged in clinical practice. Having said that, very few of us put our hand in a fire more than once, and although this one instance *might* create scarring, it certainly succeeds in behavioral change. So, as always,

I recommend people make choices for themselves.

Some may argue that people should be naturally motivated to do the right thing, in this case, take responsibility around the house and "pull their weight." However, if we scratch beneath the surface, those who make such an argument are often the ones who *do* feel rewarded for pulling their weight. The reward for them is that of avoiding negative appraisal of others or perhaps feeling a sense of accomplishment for doing their part. Those people have an intrinsic motivator for "pulling their weight," whereas others do not have this intrinsic motivation as they do not fear or acknowledge any possible negative appraisal of others and feel no reward or accomplishment for taking out the rubbish. In fact, they find it more rewarding to sit on the couch (the reasons for this often also lie in their childhood development).

Keep it simple: People are motivated by rewards and punishments.

Ramifications of Blame and Responsibility

I have mostly focused on how blame and responsibility play out in an individual and, subsequently, how they can impact their relationships and success as they navigate the adult world. However, this dynamic also plays out on larger scales. I have made mention of it playing out in a company that lacks responsibility as it seeks profit, but it can equally play out on a scale of a nation with irresponsible or selfish leaders or across a culture as its people all gradually slip into acceptance of bad, selfish or irresponsible behavior. Such things can play out much easier than one might first think. A skilled Blamer/Avoider can deflect blame and convince others that someone else is at fault. If such individuals are placed at the helm of a company or government, they can eventually persuade the population that the fault lies not with them but with a rival company, government, or even the population itself. They will avoid taking responsibility, distribute blame, and then instigate some change to distract the people from realizing what really happened. Much like that child who broke the window, blamed their sibling, and then tried to distract their mother by talking about something else that needed her attention. Only in this case, it's not a child doing the distracting, but a highly capable and often intelligent adult who holds significantly more power and authority than their accuser.

No doubt, there are those who will reject the idea that companies or governments would act in such a way or that they would not get away with such unethical behavior. However, companies and governments seek profit and authority by nature, and it does not take long to learn that a skilled "Blamer" can help them with their goals. By taking on such individuals and exchanging their well-meaning ideals for an assured victory, they inadvertently start this process of avoiding responsibility for short-term gain. This is the dynamic of shirking responsibility or development in preference for short-term gains, achieved only through the victimization of others. There is no growth or development in such an organization; it will repeat its blaming and avoidant ways and never improve its skill sets or capabilities. This may well result in short-term power and wealth. However, given enough time, it is destined to collapse, much like a child who opts for blame and avoidance will inevitably struggle in adulthood. Human history is littered with examples of nations that failed due to their lack of ability to take responsibility and make choices that required short-term sacrifice for long-term prosperity.

The Takeaway

Realize that avoiding responsibility is a sign you are avoiding what you fear, a judgment, or a suggestion that you are not good enough. Once a person realizes that they are good enough regardless of their mistake, they can accept the mistake, learn from it, and become better than they were moments before. Refuse to accept you are good enough, and you are likely to avoid this responsibility and miss the opportunity to improve as a person. Ironically, your attempt to protect the idea that you are good enough by not admitting fault is what prevents you from developing into something better and developing the belief that you are, in fact, good enough.

By taking responsibility for our actions, we place ourselves in a position to learn from mistakes, make adjustments, and improve ourselves. Equally, if we take responsibility for ourselves, we prevent others from having to suffer in some way, and we show consideration for others while simultaneously protecting ourselves from a possible negative appraisal from others.

Keep it simple: Being aware of how your actions impact you and others will help you know when to take responsibility for yourself. This requires considering the consequences.

Responsibility is a process, ideally one that starts in our early childhood and gradually develops over time. It is born of a loving, supportive, and nurturing environment that does not shy away from making a child face their fears. It also builds one's self-awareness providing them with an accurate understanding of their abilities and limitations. With this, a person can know themselves and what to expect of themselves in any given situation. This will, in essence, provide them with a sense of certainty, which gives them confidence in themselves. This confidence is the antithesis of anxiety, a cure for it, shall we say, for no one is ever anxious and confident at the same time.

Perhaps this process of developing responsibility in adulthood can be simplified to removing your pride or holding your courage long enough to accept and take responsibility for your imperfection. Learn to become comfortable with this initial discomfort and choose to improve upon yourself with humility and acceptance. Over time, you'll seek responsibility as a way to see just how far you can go.

Pushing through that initial discomfort, or instant "pain," is a vital and perhaps the most difficult step. But by doing so, we put ourselves on the path of progress. It is a classic case of short-term pain for long-term gain or instant versus delayed gratification. By choosing to delay gratification, we get onto the path of taking responsibility and improving ourselves rather than the short-term gain of avoiding responsibility and feeling "safe." This process is made easier by understanding that by taking the possible pain of responsibility now, you will reap the rewards later, such as self-esteem, confidence, greater success, and greater depth of adult functioning as you face everything that life throws at you.

Keep it simple: The process of developing responsibility in adulthood is made easier by believing or knowing that the delayed positive reinforcement will override any instant negative sensation. This dynamic of instant versus delayed gratification is a theme that runs through all of life, not least of all the development of one's sense of responsibility.

Responsibility in a nutshell

- short-term discomfort
- improved awareness of actions and choices
- difficulty in putting effort towards self-improvement
- less disapproval from self and others due to skill development
- increased self-esteem or confidence due to skill development
- reduced anxiety, leading to reduced negative self-appraisal
- improved predictability of outcomes by knowing one's capabilities and limits
- increased certainty of outcomes
- increased security and happiness.

Keep it simple: Taking responsibility leads to confidence and improved levels of happiness while being somewhat of an antidote for anxiety, fear, and self-doubt.

Chapter 6 – Factor 2: The Primary Pitfall

Another common factor that presents itself in clinical practice, and in general, is what I call the Primary Pitfall. People often say things such as, "I didn't expect that of them," or "I can't understand why you would do that!" Essentially, they have had an interaction with someone that resulted in surprise or confusion; they did not see it coming. This can be a singular event, or it can be something that happens over the course of time. Either way, the person is left confused. They cannot work out why someone would behave in the way they did. The reason for this is not because confused people lack intelligence but because they lack a broader understanding of human nature. More specifically, they lack insight into the fact that not all of us play by the same rules, ethics, or morals. We fail to predict an action because it is not an action we would ever take, and so we do not foresee it happening; we wrongly assume that others are like us. This phenomenon is more commonly known as the mirror image bias, however it seems not to be all that commonly known at all.

In its simplest terms, the Primary Pitfall (or mirror image bias) is assuming others are like us and that they share the same rule book on behavior. We assume that they have the same "spirit of intent" that we do. This, in turn, limits us from considering other possible options that exist. Another way of viewing this is the failure to understand the "true agenda" of others. By assuming others are as we are, we automatically apply our morals, ethics, and expectations to others. When they behave differently, we are surprised or confused as to "how" a person could behave in such a way.

Our failure to predict their behavior, or our surprise at their behavior, is due more to our inability to understand the vast scope of human nature than it is to this other person doing anything surprising. In fact, to them, they are acting as expected, and it is you who is the "crazy" person by reacting as you did.

The biggest impact of the Primary Pitfall is when it comes from someone who very much seems like us but has some very different core tenants. For example, a hardened, lifelong, violent, and murderous criminal is likely to look and act very differently to a lifelong humanitarian volunteer. Place these two people in a room together, and they may or may not get along, but they will realize fairly quickly that they are different people with different values. As such, they are unlikely to fall into this Primary Pitfall as they can see there are differences and are unlikely to be surprised by the other person's views or behaviors. This is not to say that they could predict the other's views or actions, but at the very least, they are unconsciously open to understanding that this person is very different and to expect the unexpected.

The problem arises when the other person appears very similar to us. When there is little obvious difference, or when there is apparent alignment in views across the two. We start to automatically expect that they are like us. Once we reach this point, we are often less vigilant towards our differences, or we explain them away, placing us in a position of *expecting* them to be just like us. We have essentially failed to see the differences and should this core difference suddenly and strongly present itself, we will be blindsided by it. We are confused as to how and what happened, and our minds are convinced we know what to expect of this person. We were not expecting the unexpected.

As human beings in any society, we develop a set of implicit rules or understanding around how that society functions and what to expect of others. We often tell stories to children that hold these implicit rules or expectations, or perhaps in music or celebrations. Perhaps the most generally accepted rule in current Western culture is that we do not roam the streets murdering and pillaging at will. We are all taught from a young age that hurting others is wrong, and therefore, we are, for the most part, trained not to. We see this in books, TV shows, or even in the family home when one child punches or kicks the other for taking their toy. Some authority will state and enforce this idea that harming others is not acceptable and is punishable in some way. At the extreme end of harming others, we have extreme repercussions, and so it is burned into our psyche that killing is wrong. Along with this learning also comes the learning that we also expect not to be killed as we go about our day. And for the most part, this expectation is upheld, as thankfully, the vast majority of us do not get killed or assaulted as we do our shopping.

From this constant teaching and enforcement, the brain simply assumes that because we would not kill someone, then others also would not kill us. It's a reasonable assumption, and there is a strong argument for the idea that people tend not to crave murder and violence as they collect their groceries. The default here is that a person "assumes" that their spirit of intent, in this case, non-violence, is shared by those around them, so everyone in that grocery store is simply "intending" to get their groceries and go about their day. Furthermore, no one in that grocery store is actively considering assaulting someone.

The primary assumption is that "People think like me" or, more accurately, "People have the same spirit of intent as I do." However, this is not an accurate assumption. It might be reasonable to assume that the people in that store are there to get their groceries in a calm and orderly fashion. After all, you were likely raised in the same society or local community. In reality, you do not know that that person would not run you down with their shopping trolley to get the last can of tomatoes. In fact, it is entirely possible that the only reason they do not terrorize you in that grocery store is because it will result in them getting caught, punished, and failing to get home with the tomatoes. They may well act as you do, but it may not be for the same reasons.

Although it might be reasonable to expect that most people in that grocery store have a similar spirit of intent in getting groceries, that is all that would be reasonable to say. We are only able to see the surface action or "act" rather than any underlying reasons for that act.

For those struggling to believe that someone might climb over you to get that tin of tomatoes, one only has to look at the chaos of grocery stores during times of shortage, when people's agendas are pushed to the surface.

I have used an extreme case of violence here to paint a picture and hopefully sear the image into your memory. However, this same concept applies to any human desire, action, or belief. Instead of violence, we could use greed, gratitude, care, or any other human trait. You may assume that someone is showing consideration when they let you go ahead of them in a queue, and you may assume that makes them a considerate person. But they may have let you go ahead simply because they are avoiding returning home to their partner. Their primary intent was towards *themselves,* not you. They did show consideration, but their primary intent may be avoidance. The scenarios are endless, and we cannot know for absolute certainty why people do what they do. We can only assume, or perhaps ask, to determine their motives, and that assumes they are honest in their reports of their motives. Typically, we observe people over long periods of time and come to "know" their motives. As stated earlier, this is never certain and is based on assumptions. It is when these assumptions surprisingly prove to be wrong that we stumble into that Primary Pitfall.

Let's explore this grocery store example. Anyone who has done their fair share of grocery shopping will have come across the person who is always trying to speed past you to get to the milk you are both heading towards. They may cut in front of you with their trolley without care or even awareness of your presence. Others may have reached for the last bottle of milk and then noticed you looking at it, only to then hand you that last bottle. You are all there to get groceries, and you share that spirit of intent; however, there are also other, deeper underlying dynamics at play.

In this example, there are three people grocery shopping. One is primarily there to fill their needs, another is willing to sacrifice their needs for the benefit of others, and the third is you. So, the spirit of intent is the same—getting groceries—but it is different from the person's underlying "values." One values their needs above others, the other values someone else's needs over their own, and it is likely that all three are assuming the other two have the same basic approach as they do. This may seem an innocuous example, but then so is the setting. It is the concept that matters and one that becomes far more important when the setting is changed.

The Primary Pitfall can often result in someone ending up in therapy, not because of an exchange in a grocery store, but because of a far more meaningful exchange in a relationship, typically with an intimate partner or close family member. Falling into the Primary Pitfall while grocery shopping will have little to no impact, but failing to see something coming from a significant other? That is grounds for significant psychological distress and injury.

Let's take the case of you being in an intimate relationship. You will have certain underlying expectations or beliefs about what that means, how you should behave towards each other, and how it will impact the course of your life. Some of these expectations might include monogamy, trust, safety, supporting each other, shared responsibilities, and so on. There is also some understanding or expectation of the trajectory of a relationship. In the early dating stage, there may be few expectations around things such as frequency of contact or exclusivity. However, once that relationship has progressed to marriage and children, it is far more reasonable to expect your partner to be involved in your daily life and help care for the children. In fact, should the relationship have progressed to that point, it is likely that you both shared the understanding that a relationship *does*, in fact, progress beyond dating.

So, how does this relate to the Primary Pitfall leading someone into the therapy room? Well, let's take the example of: "I can't understand why he would cheat on me! I would never do that to him!"

Clearly, in a situation such as that, the cheating itself is a major contributor to their distress. But then there are also those who *did* see it coming, and although distressed about what it means for their relationship, they are not shocked to have learned of the cheating. They saw it coming and knew it was possible. They did not assume that just because they themselves would not cheat, this also applied to their partner, so their overall distress is measurably less.

Countless times, I have seen clients who were either surprised by their spouse cheating on them or "expected as much." It is this second group that had insight into the Primary Pitfall. They realized that although they themselves would never cheat, this does not necessarily mean that their partner would not. Although they are hurt by the action, they do not have to go through the added step of trying to understand how it was possible.

Disclaimer: to be clear, the Primary Pitfall is about one's failure to consider or understand another person's agenda and how this can contribute to your own shock or psychological injury. It does not justify others' bad behavior but rather explains why that behavior may be more impactful for those who fall into this pitfall, as opposed to those who can see or understand the behavior even though they disapprove of it.

Keep it simple: The Primary Pitfall is assuming that others are similar to us, acting for the same reasons and following the same rules, morals, ethics, or expectations.

It is perhaps the more subtle things that are difficult to see coming. Violence and infidelity are concepts that we are all aware of and, to some extent, understand or at least know that they occur. The human traits or actions that are less understood tend to be the most confusing for those falling into this pitfall. Take, for example, *social status*. This is not an unknown concept, but it's also not one that we most actively consider. A person (let's say the wife) may be confused as to why their husband is far more kind, considerate, interactive, funny, etc., when they are out with a group of friends as opposed to at home with the family. One might expect that a person should treat their family better than they treat anyone else, and yet there are those who are far more generous and engaging with friends, co-workers, or even strangers. The reason for this is that although the husband has these mentioned traits, his drive to play them out is based on wanting acceptance or elevation from others. It is not that he is considerate by nature. It is that he has learned consideration can advance him socially, and so he displays that trait. The underlying reason is selfishness and personal gain. The wife, however, may well be considerate by nature rather than enacting it for personal gain. She simply assumes her husband is the same; after all, he did display consideration for her for many years prior to their having a family. It may never have occurred to her that he was doing this to consolidate a family for himself. For this reason, it is difficult for her to accept the true motives of his actions. She has spent years being convinced he held different motives, ones that are the same as hers. And so, she has fallen into the Primary Pitfall.

Keep it simple: Failing to understand the reasons for one's behavior can lead us to make false assumptions about the motive of that behavior. If a surface behavior is similar or the same as ours, we tend to assume it comes from the same motives we hold for that behavior. We can find ourselves in this pitfall when their behaviors seem out of character, but in fact, it is that we misunderstand their character and assume it is similar to ours.

In order to reduce the chances of falling into this pitfall, we first have to be aware of the entire scope of human nature. Most of us tend to live within a small subset of what humans are capable of. For example, anyone who spends any time with others tends to show a degree of politeness most days. Most of us don't show the "killer instinct" of a professional fighter intent on hurting their opponent to win their fight. If you place an ordinary person into a boxing ring, they may throw some punches, but often, they are not thrown with full force; there is no underlying blood lust driving them to knock the opponent out. This is because they do not, or have not, explored and embraced that part of their human nature. I would argue that, generally speaking, everyone is capable of the full spectrum of human nature, but only if the circumstance is right. Most of us tend to be limited to a small portion of that spectrum.

Most people can show kindness, be it genuine or forced; some can show true selflessness, and few can show complete self-sacrifice for total strangers. Some abhor the con artist who scams people of their life savings, while others see it as a battle of intelligence, and if they can con another, then they have earned that money. Such a con artist has no consideration for what happens to their victim; their only concern is their own personal gain and perhaps the battle of wits. Such a con artist likely has a greater understanding of the spectrum of human nature. They understand the kindness of their victim, and they understand the depth of selfishness that is possible when focusing solely on your own gain. The victim, however, has little to no understanding of what others, such as this con artist, are capable of, as they only live within their small subset of human nature.

Keep it simple: Failing to, or choosing not to, accept the full gamut of human nature will often contribute to your surprise when dealing with others and precedes the Primary Pitfall.

We can consider human nature as a continuum, with perhaps altruism on one end and pure evil on the other. Most of us will embody some section of the middle of this continuum. Some people, like those dedicated to helping others, tend to consistently reside closer to the altruism scale and not deviate much from this, while others may lean towards altruism while also being able to access a violent side if needed. The con artist in the above scenario is likely to lean more toward the evil side while also having the capacity for elements such as charm and kindness.

As human nature is rarely so clean-cut, a more thorough representation might be that of a bar graph with each bar representing a different trait of human nature. An individual can embody various traits of human nature without there needing to be a complete embodiment of all the traits in between.

No Pitfall: Correct Assumption and the Same Spirit of Intent

Let's explore a scenario where there is no pitfall and why. Take an early-stage relationship. If you both share the same spirit of intent to get to know each other, hopefully fall in love, and live happily ever after, then you are off to a good start. Your spirit of intent is the same, as is your surface expectation from the onset. Over time, as you both grow in your understanding of your partner's intentions, morals, ethics, or otherwise, what areas of human nature they lean towards and are capable of, you become less likely to be surprised. You are less likely to be a victim of the Primary Pitfall as you know what to expect, and this knowledge is not based on assumption but on observation and understanding.

To take it a step further, the more aware you are of what human nature is capable of, the better you can identify certain traits, such as an undesired narcissist partner, before becoming emotionally attached. Keep in mind, of course, that everyone has the capacity to exhibit a range of behaviors if and when required.

I am not convinced that we can ever be entirely sure about how a person is going to behave. However, the better we know or understand them, what section of the human nature scale they tend to inhabit, and what agendas they have, the more likely we are to accurately predict their behaviors and character. This understanding comes with time, as the person learns and observes, but it is also helped by understanding human nature more broadly to know what to look for and what is possible that you had never considered. The key here is that you are understanding them, who they are, and what they are likely to do. Importantly, you are not projecting *your* values or agenda onto them but rather reading their agenda and values for what they are, independent of your own.

Keep it simple: Protect against falling into the Primary Pitfall by being aware of the entire scope of human nature and observing the other person without projecting your values, agendas, or personal views onto them. Don't make assumptions, only observations, and remember, it's not about you.

It is when we fail to do this that we "assume" that a person will behave or act in a way similar to us or in a way we might expect that we are at risk of falling into this pitfall. At first, this may seem obvious, but it's surprising how often this plays out, both in short- and long-term interactions with others.

Clear Pitfall: Projection and Misidentifying the Spirit of Intent

Now, let's say you want a long-term relationship, but the other person has no intent of long-term commitment. Depending on the circumstances of your meeting (online, in person, via friends, etc.), it is entirely possible that you were both justified in assuming the other wanted the same thing you did. Both people are likely to show their interest by being flirtatious with one another. The person seeking something long-term takes this as a positive sign of interest and a good start to a meaningful relationship. Equally, this is seen as a good sign by the party seeking something short-term as it directs things towards advancing quickly and is in line with their desires. Both parties see what they want to see, and the stronger their hope or desire for their own needs is, the longer they will see what they want to see rather than trying to determine if the other person actually wants the same thing they do. This is not a case of either party trying to actively deceive the other, but rather a genuine misunderstanding of the other, usually due to following their own strong desires or hopes.

People can become very fixated on their desires or points of view. We unconsciously want what we want, or perhaps want to be "right," so we funnel all our beliefs into our own views or desires rather than stopping to consider what the other party wants or intends. Only when we let go of this personal agenda do we start to see things more accurately. Often, it's by letting go of our "wants" and having those difficult and direct conversations we'd rather avoid that we begin to see things more clearly.

In this scenario, it is a case of both people having different intents and their *hope* that the other wants the same thing as they do, which can temporarily blind them to the other person's real intent. How temporary this is depends on how willing they are to sideline their own hopes and look at things more objectively. Many have heard the classic statements such as "Love is blind" or "I can't believe I didn't see it!" We walk ourselves into the Primary Pitfall because our hope is greater than our tolerance to face a reality that we may not like. Projecting our hopes or agendas onto others isn't limited to relationships. It can occur in many areas, such as *hoping* a fad diet will work, believing a new product will make us attractive, trusting an investment is as good as the salesperson claims, and so on.

Keep it simple: Ultimately, there is a greater chance of the Primary Pitfall when there is a difference in the spirit of intent between two people, especially when communication is not clear and one's hopes outweigh their tolerance for disappointment.

Once a person realizes they have fallen into the pitfall of assuming the other person is on the same page as them, they often go through a phase of self-blame. The obvious conclusion to them is that they were *stupid* for not seeing it or for ignoring it. This is a natural response, but ideally, it is a stage they do not spend too much time in, or they risk further damaging their self-esteem and belief in their judgment. Ideally, they can soon shift from self-blame to responsibility and self-compassion. Once they realize it was their better nature that led them down that path of blindness, they can start to consider what they learned from the experience, how much more of that scale of human nature they are now aware of, and how they're armed to do better next time. If they can do this and not put a negative bias on their positive traits, then they can recover and not allow the now-removed partner to continue to take from them.

Led Pitfall: The Narcissist Partner

One of the most striking times that the Primary Pitfall presents itself is when a person unknowingly enters into a relationship with a narcissist (or even a sociopath). A narcissist does a great job of appearing like a regular person. They are often charming, intelligent, and very socially capable. This is why they often go undetected at first and sometimes for months or years. They do a great job of blending in and knowing how to ingratiate themselves with others. They are also often a good judge of character and will use this to help them identify someone who is likely to think well of them, give them the benefit of the doubt, or be slow to call them out on their behaviors. In some ways, they are choosing someone who is likely to fall into the Primary Pitfall. Someone who is very unlike them, therefore, does not naturally consider narcissistic behavior as an explanation or even understand what a narcissist is.

Once the narcissist has selected a *safe* or *easy* target, they have a buffer to work with. There will be a time lag between the narcissist weaving their controlling web and the target realizing it is happening. The poor target has no idea of what they are in for, largely because they have never come across this part of human nature and are blind to it. In fact, they see things through their own kind, forgiving eyes and tend to explain away or dismiss any idea of the narcissist doing wrong. At times, they may go as far as accepting the narcissist did something wrong, but they are "working on getting better," which, of course, they are not. If anything, they are working on getting better at blindsiding and taking advantage of them. But again, the target person would never conceive of this being something a person would do, so they are also blind to this.

When the narcissist starts exerting control over the relationship, they assume this is just because he/she "knows what they want" or because "they are driven." When the narcissist starts telling them what to wear or who they can spend time with, it can be explained away as "wanting what's best for me, so I look nice," or "so that I don't fall in with the wrong crowd."

These *explanations* for the narcissist's behavior are reasonable ones to make. After all, we do not want to think negatively of our partner, so we assume the best and attribute a kind perspective to it. We do this because we have probably put ourselves in their position and try to understand why we would do something like that to our partner. "Why would I override my partner's life choice like that? Well, *I* would only do that if I had a good reason that would benefit us both. I must know something they don't or be more driven. That is the only reason *I* would act like that, so that must be why *they* are acting like that."

The logic here is sound. The average person is just trying to make sense of things and putting themselves in someone else's shoes is a good way to go about that. However, it is all based on the assumption that *others* think or act as *we* do. We assume that they hold our values, beliefs, morals, and understanding of how to be human beings. This is the essence of the Primary Pitfall: the failure to consider the whole spectrum of what humans are capable of and what other reasons there may be behind their actions.

If, after reading the last few paragraphs, you find yourself thinking that's a bit much and people aren't like that, then you may well be a prime target for a narcissist. And if, after reading the above, you find yourself thinking, "Yeah, that's true. I see this all the time. There are so many narcissists out there," then you have likely not only come across a narcissist but may have possibly been damaged by them to the point of having your bias skewed too far in the other direction. Although narcissists do exist, they are far from the bulk of the population. A 2008 study found the rate of narcissism to be around 6.2% in the general

US population, with greater rates in men (7.7%) than women (4.8%) (Stinson et al., 2008), although it certainly does seem as though the world is creating more narcissists by the day.

Most people have never learned about narcissism, let alone how to identify the signs of it in others, and as such, they are not armed with the knowledge to realize what they are facing. We approach others with our own explanations for their behavior based on our own experience of how to be a human. Is it any wonder people get so confused and wrapped up by these narcissists?

How could any of us accurately understand what a bird perched in a tree thinks of us if we have never been a bird? We can only make guesses based on what *we* might think if it was *us* perched in that tree, but we have no real way to know how a bird thinks. The concept here is not understanding something we have not lived. Exchange the narcissist for a genius. Do you think you could accurately understand how and why Einstein thought as he did? What about someone who is autistic? Can you accurately understand how they think? They are human, so should we not be able to understand how and why they think as they do? The list here can go on and on, from poets to artists, dictators, and murderers.

The reality is that there is a broad scope of traits and possibilities that cover human nature. Most of us inhabit a small "normal" range of this (statistically speaking), and in our rather controlled, relatively stable Western culture, we do not often see the extremes of human nature (even when it is directly in front of us). As a result, our brains are not accustomed to considering the extremes as possibilities, and due to this lack of exposure or understanding of the extremes, we are very unskilled in correctly understanding the reasons behind others' actions. We simply assume they do things for the reasons we do them.

Consider this: when you walk past or interact with a person, you often perceive them as "normal" like yourself. It's only when you discover or are told about their differences—whether they're autistic, a criminal, or anything else—that you begin to understand their unique perspectives.

If someone acted rudely to you while you still believed they were just like you, you might label them as rude or selfish. However, if you knew from the start that they were autistic and perhaps unaware of certain social norms, you would more likely see their behavior as a misunderstanding rather than intentional rudeness. It's similar to not expecting someone in a wheelchair to stand up to greet you. Recognizing and considering these differences helps us better understand others' actions.

Keep it simple: When we can't easily identify how a person is different, we tend to expect them to be the same. This gives us a false belief of what to expect from others, and we are more prone to being blindsided.

If we are not aware of this broad range of human nature, we cannot begin to factor it into our perspective of others. If we become aware of it, we need to be able to accurately identify a person's nature, motives, agendas, beliefs, etc. Only once we can do this do we place ourselves in a position of being aware of what we are in for with another person. Thankfully, people are more alike than not, and we tend to gravitate to a social norm. However, there are enough people that this pitfall is a relatively common occurrence.

In a way, because most of us are poor at identifying things such as pathological greed or narcissism, we do not realize that the person we voted for in the last election was probably both. We assumed they were what they said they were, dedicated to making our society better. But in truth, any deviant who wants power knows enough to say such things and also knows that as long as they present well, the majority of decent, well-meaning people in the world will believe them because they want to believe them. When a politician is elected despite lying, they are essentially rewarded for their deceit, encouraging them to continue this behavior. Many people fail to notice the lie even years later, allowing this bad behavior to go unpunished. The average well-meaning person lacks the desire to revisit and address these past deceptions; they just want to move on with their lives. This lack of accountability further encourages politicians or narcissists to persist in their dishonest acts, as their actions are either unnoticed or unpunished.

Keep it simple: Human nature spans a broad spectrum from good to evil and everything in between. Most of us inhabit a narrow segment of this spectrum and wrongly believe our experience is the full range. As we have no idea the rest of the range exists, we struggle to see it, let alone understand it. The broader your understanding of human nature, the better equipped you are to avoid being blindsided by it.

Narcissists understand the manipulative side of humanity, and through their keen observation of others, they also understand the kind side. This gives them an advantage in any human exchange because they understand that their target does *not* understand them. It's an unfair fight; the target is not just bringing a knife to a gunfight—they don't even realize they're in a fight. Meanwhile, the narcissist is armed with both a knife and a gun.

This scenario of a narcissist manipulating a good person via a relationship is not an uncommon one. I have had numerous clients present with symptoms of anxiety, self-doubt, and low self-esteem, only to find that this has developed due to being in a relationship with a narcissist. In most cases, they still have little to no insight into the fact that their partner is a narcissist, even 2–3 years into the relationship, often as they have continued to explain away their partner's behaviors using the framework of what they themselves would do. They struggle to—or do not want to—admit that their partner is simply rude, selfish, and narcissistic. Why would they? They have just invested years of their lives into this relationship. No one wants to admit they have made a bad investment. To top it off, they have also developed a habit of defending their narcissistic partner. The narcissist will undoubtedly have attacked them for not jumping to their defense when a friend or family member called them out on their narcissistic actions. The narcissist has trained their target to be their defender.

What can be said for a person in this situation is that they are often *good* people. They are forever trying to find the good in their partner. They are forgiving, tolerant, and committed to making their relationship work. This is exactly what you want in a partner, and this was not lost on the narcissist when they pursued this person in the first instance. Should this partner be able to pull themselves away from the narcissist and do so without too much injury, those same traits place them in excellent stead for a functional relationship. All they need to do is not fall for another narcissist and not let the mistreatment they suffered be projected onto their new, non-narcissist partner.

Keep it simple: A person's nature shapes their expectations of others: a kind and reasonable person assumes others will be the same, while a devious and selfish person expects others to be like them.

Essentially, the kind person gives the benefit of the doubt, while the unkind person is cautious of being taken advantage of while also trying to take advantage of others. This tends to play out in such a way that the kind person keeps giving while the unkind person keeps taking. The kind person goes in innocently, while the unkind person goes in ready to profit in some way. This ultimately leads to the kind person being hurt and the unkind person not believing their luck as they continue to benefit. This is sometimes referred to as "taking advantage," "emotional abuse," or "sales".

The damage that a narcissistic person can do to another is quite extensive; they can take years of someone's life and leave their victim reeling for many years to come. The emotional damage caused can lead a person's life to derail for decades, especially in the case of narcissistic parents targeting their children. They commonly rob others of their time, money, and mental well-being. This damage can be exponentially amplified in the case of a narcissistic company rather than a narcissistic individual. A company with a narcissistic culture (or simply narcissistic leadership) tends to have no care for the negative impacts of its actions and focuses only on how it can profit from the *gullible* masses. Interestingly, narcissists are more represented in high-level executive positions than they are in the general population, which leads one to wonder what drives large company's promotion processes or selection criteria.

Returning to the earlier grocery store example, we assume that the person rushing ahead of you to get the last carton of milk has done so due to being selfish and not caring about pushing past you. Although this is a definite possibility, we cannot know that for sure. They could be a narcissist simply doing what narcissists do, they could be so mentally preoccupied they did not even notice you, or they might be in a high state of anger due to some issue that morning. We can only guess about someone's mindset. While assuming they are selfish or rude might seem obvious or likely, it's still just an assumption. How we choose to interpret their behavior impacts our feelings and reactions. If we assume they are rude or out to get us, our day turns negative. But if we assume they are having a bad day or simply don't know better, we can adopt an understanding, forgiving, or even grateful mindset. After all, our day has been kinder to us than theirs has been to them.

Keep it simple: It is those who seem most like us who will surprise us most when they act differently.

Blindside Pitfall: Failing to Identify the Spirit of Intent

Whereas the previous clear pitfall scenario is a case of flawed communication or observation leading to a genuine misunderstanding of what each other wanted, blindsided pitfall is that of purposeful misleading. This is where the other party deliberately misleads you into

CHAPTER 6 – FACTOR 2: THE PRIMARY PITFALL

thinking your assumption of them is correct, when they know full well it is not. This is where you want that long-term relationship, and the other party *knows* this but wants only a one-night affair. However, they also know that admitting this will likely lead to them not getting what they want, so they very convincingly say and do everything they can to convince you they, too, want that long-term relationship. They will continue to do this right up until their desires are met. This could be that they then abandon you after the first sexual interaction, or it may be that they string this along for as long as it serves their needs.

The common argument here would be, "Well, this isn't failing to identify the spirit of intent. It is them lying and cheating." And yes, this is certainly part of it. However, in most cases, those who end up the victim of the above scenario are the ones who would never have considered acting as their "lying partner" did. You see, the victim in this scenario likely never considered that the other person was lying, and certainly not after they convincingly said and did all the right things. This is because they themselves would not dream of spending weeks or months feeding into a lie of a relationship simply to get some base desire filled. They likely see this as a waste of time and effort that would be better put towards just honestly seeking a partner that wanted the same thing. The Primary Pitfall here is assuming the other person thinks the way you do or has the same spirit of intent as you. It's quite possible that all they really wanted was the satisfaction of deceiving someone.

The victim here does not consider that the other person *enjoys* fooling them and having their way with them, seeing how long they can keep them fooled. The victim also tends to assume that the other person would feel bad for causing so much pain and hurt when, in fact, they have absolutely no concern for the victim's feelings whatsoever. If this proves hard for you to accept, then you are likely a good person and, sadly, more at risk of the Primary Pitfall. Again, you would probably feel bad or guilty about hurting someone because you avoid behaving that way. However, not everyone shares your perspective. Your belief that hurting others is wrong may stem from your upbringing and is likely common in your community but not universal. Remember, assuming others think or behave like you can lead to misunderstandings.

So, in this blindside pitfall example, yes, the other person has lied and cheated in order to convince you of something. You are convinced by their deceptive comments and actions and believe their spirit of intent is the same as yours; however, it was only ever one of selfish desire. Such a scenario can be difficult to process and recover from as your mind has to grapple with not just having been taken advantage of and the obvious pain associated with that but also the concept that evil people exist, and you just had a close encounter with one.

Keep it simple: Actions that cause you guilt may cause others a sense of pride or achievement.

It can be challenging for many to accept that some people, especially those who are naturally kind, may refuse to believe that others lack empathy or consideration for others' feelings and well-being. However, the reality is that such individuals do exist, and they always have. Clinically, these people are often referred to as sociopathic. There's a significant body of research on these personality types known as "The Dark Triad," which delves deeper into understanding them. If you're interested in learning more about these personality types, exploring this topic could be worthwhile.

Commonality of the Pitfall

One thing to keep in mind, especially for those struggling to accept this reality of humanity, is that these sociopathic types are a minority in the world. It is also important to remember that, for the most part, this Primary Pitfall often occurs on the milder scale, which is not to suggest that it does not have significant impacts on mood and anxiety levels. The more common case of the Primary Pitfall is not the one that occurs when dealing with a sociopath (those are just the obvious and expensive cases) but when dealing with one's own denial or lack of consideration of others. The Pitfall more often occurs when you have failed to remove yourself from your own internal world and expectations and really consider the other person and their motives. Do not confuse this with some veiled "victim blaming." One's own failure to honestly and genuinely consider the other person by removing one's own self-expectations is often the precursor to the Primary Pitfall. It is often the kind or "nice" people who are more susceptible.

The idea that you have contributed to the pitfall rather than falling into an unseen trap is easily understood by anyone who has experienced a failed relationship. How often do we ignore early warning signs of a bad relationship? How many times has a friend pointed out an issue only for us to dismiss it, convincing ourselves it isn't a problem? Have you ever looked back and thought, "How did I miss that?" We often overlook these signs because our hope overrides our better judgment. Initially, we assume the person is like us and ignore signs that they are not.

While some might view this as a foolish error, it can also reflect a more virtuous aspect of humanity. It shows hope for others, a belief in the best in people, and a willingness to overlook imperfections. Perhaps the line between kindness and foolishness is the extent of one's chosen blindness. Educating people about human nature and implementing consequences for bad interpersonal behavior might help avoid such pitfalls.

Anxiety and the Primary Pitfall

Anxiety also plays an underlying role in falling into the Primary Pitfall. Our desire for safety and certainty unconsciously drives many of our behavioral choices. Therefore, we *want* to believe that our understanding of humanity and people in general is accurate. If our understanding or expectation of others is accurate, then we can predict how our interactions with others will play out. This gives us a clearer and more certain view of our future. We assume others think and act like us, believing that if we don't do bad things, others won't either. This desire for safety is strong and can often prevent us from considering alternatives.

Additionally, it's mentally easier not to question our thoughts. Challenging our thinking requires effort, and it's simpler to assume others are like us. We also have a natural tendency to want to be right, so we look for evidence that supports our beliefs (confirmation bias) and ignore signs that contradict them. When we realize we're wrong, we experience a spike of anxiety as our brain tries to regain an understanding of a situation. We would rather avoid this spike of anxiety and so lie to ourselves to prevent it from entering our reality.

Avoiding the Primary Pitfall

The key to avoiding the Primary Pitfall is to have an accurate perception of humanity and what others are capable of while not entering the realm of paranoia. There is a balance of trust and caution. Taking the paranoid stance that everyone is out to get you, and they have to prove otherwise, will likely lead to you being very defensive and standoffish, signaling to others that you have trust issues. Conversely, blindly trusting everyone on every level will only signal that you are an easy target for those few who are looking for an easy win for themselves.

Firstly, be aware of the pitfall but not to the point of paranoia or expectation that others will coax you into the pit. Rather, it is entirely in the realm of possibility that others do not think, act, or feel as you do, at least not on everything.

Secondly, figure out the other person's agenda. We all have an agenda, which is not an inherently negative thing but simply a reality. Doing good for the world, for example, is a positive agenda, but an agenda nonetheless.

To improve your accuracy in identifying someone else's agenda, you first must be aware of your own inner drives. This is to say you need to understand why you think, feel, act, and react as you do. This may not be easy for everyone, but it is something that can be made simpler via reflection, introspection, and perhaps psychotherapy. Once you have a reasonable grasp on this, it is far easier to set your own agenda aside and consider the other person without your own biases. When you are

CHAPTER 6 – FACTOR 2: THE PRIMARY PITFALL

free of your psychological vices and emotional tendencies, you will be able to consider the other person more clearly. You will learn to ask the questions you may not want to hear answers to and observe their behaviors in their entirety rather than filter them through your hopes. You will see where their words and actions align and where they do not. You will listen to and understand their history and be able to infer more accurately what their underlying drives, desires, values, and intents are. By seeing these things, you will have more insight into what their agenda really is and if it aligns with what they say it is.

Practically, you could always ask yourself, "Why else might they have said or done that?" This way, you're not just accepting someone's actions based on your own bias but are instead considering other possible explanations. Over time, as you learn the truth, you can see if your initial instinct or your second guess was more accurate.

However, be careful not to overthink this. There are countless reasons for any action, and over-analyzing can lead to anxiety and neuroticism. Just consider one alternative explanation, and don't give it too much weight until you have enough evidence to prove or disprove it.

Finally, be aware of the whole spectrum of human behavior and emotion. Be aware of the extremes that humanity is capable of. Do not limit your understanding of humanity to just the people you have known throughout your life. Consider figures from history who acted in unthinkable ways, both negative and positive. Consider the possibility that there exists, or did exist, a person whose life was dedicated to caring for and giving to others for no reward. Also, consider the figures that would, and have, destroyed lives by the tens of thousands and did so without a shred of guilt, remorse, or pause. Do this to realize how far the scale goes on human capability. With these fresh eyes, look at your current world. Ask yourself what the true motives and agendas are of those in the current world. You may be shocked to realize the evil around you. Preferably, you may be shocked to realize how much your friends care for you and how truly amazing those in your life and your world really are.

The Takeaway

We assume others are like us and act for the same reasons we do, which limits our understanding of human nature. This assumption makes interactions more predictable and reduces our anxiety. However, not everyone thinks or acts the same. Some people do things we could never have considered, leaving us blindsided, hurt, and confused, and even questioning our own reality.

A good person will expect others to be good, while an evil person expects others to be evil. As such, the evil person is always prepared for an attack, both towards others and towards themselves. A good person has no plan of attack and is ill-prepared to be attacked. Conversely, it is the evil person who is not prepared for any form of cooperation with others; they do not expect kindness and only see it as a sign of a new victim. The good person, however, is forever open to cooperation, friendship, and connection.

Surround a good person with good people, and they will have a safe and fulfilling life. Surround an evil person with evil people, and they will have an ongoing battle for survival with only one victor. But if you blend the two, the evil will prey upon the good until either all the good is consumed or until the good understands the evil and embraces it long enough to defeat it but not so long to be consumed by it.

It is my view that given the right set of conditions, all humans have the capacity to behave across the whole spectrum of human nature. We all have the potential for kindness or evil, and what traits emerge are a combination of one's tendencies and what their environment rewards. Most of us express a small subset of human nature and tend to expect others to inhabit that same subset. This natural and limited scope of ours can blind us to the broader range of what is possible, and so we do not understand those who inhabit a different subset of the spectrum of human nature.

Experiencing kindness shows us what kindness is, and this allows us to choose to show kindness or not. This is true for any element of human nature, such as violence, deception, love, and hatred. Most of us do not experience or even learn about certain elements of human nature, so how can we be expected to predict or even identify something we have never experienced or learned of? If you have never experienced the loss of a loved one, you will not truly understand it until it occurs. If you have never come across or learned about someone with psychosis, how can you be expected to even begin to understand it? If you have never had to fight or kill to survive, how will you know if you are capable of doing so?

Disclaimer

I want to clarify that I am not suggesting most people have nefarious agendas. While some do, it is likely a minority. However, this minority often rises to higher positions in life. In my opinion, this minority may be larger than most people think. The truly capable bad actors have learned to deceive the average person. They know how to charm and appear well-intentioned while being the proverbial wolf in sheep's clothing.

This pitfall can occur out of genuine misunderstanding, wilful blindness, or active deceit and manipulation. At times, this manipulation is not even conscious but rather a learned and unconscious adaptation to get one's needs met (often associated with past trauma or neglect and/or a personality disorder). In some ways, just as we accept the animals in their broad nature of beauty, strength, agility, and need to kill other animals, we could similarly view human nature and its ability for beauty, strength, creativity, and ability to kill or capitalize over other humans.

Chapter 7 – Factor 3: Know the Cost

This concept of "knowing the costs" is largely tied to decision-making. Time and time again during my clinical practice, a client will recount their story leading up to when their issue surfaced. At times, they can identify relatively accurately when things changed, what precipitated this, and how they feel as a consequence. They then need to consider how to accept or adapt to this. However, there are also times when they do not understand how things came to be as they are or when things started to turn for the worse.

In either case, the path that leads them to their issue (be it depression, anxiety, loss, etc.) is often not a clearly understood one. Even those clients who have largely recovered from their issues, who can accurately see where things went wrong or what they have done to correct them, will often not grasp the underlying reasons for why they arrived where they did. That is to say that they know what happened to cause or to recover from the problem but never really quite understand what exchange took place at the core of those events.

The concept here is that everything we do, and I do mean everything, will have a cost. Sometimes, this cost is high; other times, it is small, but often, it is a cost we fail to recognize or even consider. Most of us are quite aware that the decisions we make have outcomes, some good, some bad. Often, we are aware that a bad decision will cost us in some way, but we only consider this when it is an obvious cost or a big decision and fail to consider all the other associated costs.

Let's take the example of buying your first car. There is the obvious financial cost of this, but even if it was gifted to you, the cost of fuel and associated running costs still need to be considered. What else might this car cost you? Perhaps you are spending less time at home with your family and more time out in the world with friends or alone. This may be seen as a negative to your parents, who will see less of you, or perhaps they might view it as a positive! There is the potential cost that you now spend less time with your parents and therefore miss out on their wisdom or, perhaps, their abuse. You may have less time with the family dog, creating sadness for the dog. You may have less time for reading books or less time looking out of your bedroom window contemplating life. The point here is not to point out the pros or cons of the decision to buy a car but to illustrate that there are often a whole host of costs that we do not consider when making a decision.

There are far too many costs associated with any given decision to be able to consider them all—and I would not suggest anyone try. However, I do think it is important to be aware that there are often more "costs" to a decision than we realize. Perhaps it is more a question of determining which decisions have the greatest potential to have a big impact and what these impacts may be rather than favoring our inner desire to make a certain decision. Choosing how to respond to your wife or husband during a time of conflict is a great example. The decision to lash out in anger rather than showing restraint could be the reason that relationship starting down the path of hurt, resentment, and separation. This could lead to a future decision of divorce or reconciliation, either of which may be positive or negative, depending on the circumstances. The cost of choosing to lash out could well be what leads to a significant life change years into the future, which is something not often considered when arguing over day-to-day issues that every couple face.

Every decision we make has a cost or a benefit, and perhaps a mixture of the two. People often first consider how a decision benefits them. The wiser among us also weigh the costs. The wisest go further, thinking about the potential ripple effects and the subsequent costs of their decision. A person may *want* a car, and so they buy one. They have assumed an overall benefit, and they go ahead with it. However, a person may also *want* to express their frustration during conflict; they assume it's fine to do so as they are "expressing" themselves, and so they lash out rather than showing restraint. In this second example, they benefit from feeling the relief of having expressed themselves at the potential cost of hurting or losing a partner. Perhaps that was the intent, to hurt or lose the partner, in which case, the cost is also a benefit for them as they get to exit a relationship. The point here is not that one should "Make the right choice" or "Do the right thing," but rather be aware of the cost of your actions and then decide if you are willing to pay that cost.

Keep it simple: Be aware of the costs of your actions, and then decide if you are willing to pay that cost. It is not an error to pay a cost. It is an error to not know what cost you are paying.

The idea here is to bring into people's awareness that every action they take will have a cost, which in itself is not a negative thing. We happily pay the financial cost of a good meal, the time cost of completing a task we enjoy or obtain a reward from, or the energy cost of exercising. Cost should not be seen as an inherently negative thing but an inevitable thing. The question is: are we willing to pay that specific cost for the decision we are making? If you have a good idea of what the costs of your actions might be, then you are in a better position to know if you are willing to pay that cost. However, if you do not know what the costs may be, then you are playing a game of chance with your decisions. You may get lucky, and the cost turns out to be minimal (your partner does not take your lashing out personally and promptly forgives you), or you may get unlucky (and you lose your partner, home, kids, and social connections). Again, the error is not the action itself; it is failing to properly consider the possible costs of your actions.

Keep it simple: We are unlikely to identify *all* the possible costs of any decision, but with thought and consideration, we can certainly improve our understanding of the cost of our decisions.

Let's consider the example of deciding whether to take a promotion. Most people would consider this a positive opportunity, especially if it's their first promotion offer. Generally, a promotion often results in positive life outcomes, such as a higher income and career progression. These benefits can drive one towards greater wealth, resource acquisition, and overall better life outcomes. However, promotions come with both gains and costs, including things such as mental energy as you learn the role and take on more responsibility, time as you may be required to work longer hours, and emotional impacts as stress may result from an increase in responsibility, which may impact factors such as your relationships or ability to relax. Ultimately, a good promotion, with few costs, will likely provide a net gain for your life. In contrast, a bad promotion, with many costs, might offer more wealth but at the expense of your mental health, relationships, and longevity in that field of work.

The Importance of Considered Decision-Making

The key point here is not to identify costs and decide against an action but rather to identify them and "consciously decide" if you are willing to pay those costs. In the example of buying a car, most will willingly pay those costs due to the immense gains they get from that vehicle. This concept is not presented to create fear or doubt in taking action but to reduce stress, anxiety, and internal conflict should a decision result in less-than-desirable outcomes. Keep in mind if an outcome is positive, then the costs are ignored or irrelevant. However, when the outcome is negative, we can fall into the same psychological confusion and pain as those who fall into the primary pitfall. Ultimately, you have been blindsided. How could your choice have ended so badly?! And so, the mind goes into a state of shock, confusion, and processing before it can get on with life.

Let's assume you put no thought towards the cost of that car and bought it for its ticket price. If all goes well, you will give it no more thought, and life will go on as expected. However, should that car have ongoing mechanical issues, leading to frequent repairs, you may become stressed, frustrated, angry, resentful, or even despondent every time you use it. Importantly, had you *not* considered these possibilities, your brain would be surprised by the negative outcomes. This surprise can lead to strong emotional reactions and potentially some psychological shutdown as it tries to make sense of the world. Failing to predict your world can trigger anxiety and shake your foundational understanding.

Although this example may seem trivial, consider moments when you were genuinely shocked by a friend or relative's response to your decision. Reflect on a significant loss in your life that resulted from a decision (or series of decisions) that you made. Is your kindness garnering you more friendships or leading you to bankruptcy? Are you losing friends or partners because you are being your "true/authentic self" just as you have been led to believe is the "right" thing to do? Are you failing to maintain a job and have no idea why? Do all of your relationships end in conflict and anger? Any of these (or any number of other) possible issues could well be due to your lack of consideration of the costs of your actions. Did you fail to consider that the promotion would lead to time away from your spouse, which ultimately leads to your divorce, loneliness, depression, and subsequent unemployment?

Keep it simple: Surprise around your current situation is a good indicator of a lack of consideration or knowing the costs of your past actions.

If you have at least considered as many of the costs as you can and chosen to accept them, then there is less underlying surprise or reaction *should* things go wrong. You will also be in a far better position to accept that negative outcome as your brain has some awareness and "ownership" of that outcome. One could say, "Well, I knew that could happen, I just did not expect it," which is already an advanced point of acceptance and processing compared to saying, "Wow, I had no idea that was even possible!" In the latter instance, the brain still has to process how the outcome was possible. Only then can it lead to acceptance of the event and later integration of it into one's life. This also applies to positive outcomes that were unexpected, leading to surprise and

CHAPTER 7 – FACTOR 3: KNOW THE COST

immense joy. The brain did not expect the positive outcome and may take more time for this to "sink in" before being able to accept and integrate it.

By bringing into our conscious awareness the potential costs or outcomes of our choices, we are less likely to be surprised and can fortify our minds against potential negative impacts, such as stress and anxiety.

Oftentimes, people will find themselves in therapy because they are unable to make sense of certain life events. They fail to understand and integrate an experience into their consciousness. This is partly due to their failure to "see it coming" or having failed to consider a particular cost that has eventuated.

Keep it simple: Knowing the costs not only helps make a more informed decision but also safeguards against the chance of subsequent anxiety or depression as it places the mind in a more expectant position.

We should not fear identifying the costs or sacrifices associated with any decision. Nor should we take ourselves into a negative mindset throughout this process. Everything in life has a cost; it's just a matter of identifying it and deciding if you are willing to pay it. If we are, then regardless of the outcome of the decision, we will, at worst, be disappointed but never confused or otherwise angling towards anxiety or depression. This is also due in part to the fact that once you have decided to pay a cost, you are on the path to taking responsibility for your actions regardless of the outcome.

Getting Better at Knowing the Costs

Given that knowing the costs requires a person to consider how things may play out, it might be fair to say that those with a good capacity for reflection and forethought will do well with this, as will those with significant experience with similar decisions. So how do we improve our ability to know the costs?

Firstly, simply be aware that everything has a cost. Secondly, reflect on choices you and others have made, and take the time to consider how things have played out in the past, especially the times that surprised you. Finally, consult with those who have experience, and seek out advice from those who know more or have experienced more than you have in that area. Better yet, consult with *multiple* such people.

In keeping with our theme of relationships, let's look at a common example of failing to "know the cost" of something in the setting of a relationship. After all, what's more prevalent in our lives than our relationships? I'll structure this around an intimate relationship with a partner or spouse, but the concept can translate to any relationship.

Example 1: The Engaged Couple

Let's take an engaged couple for our first example. After a two-year courtship, they decide to get engaged and move in together. At the ripe age of 25, they are full of excitement and happiness at the prospect of starting a life and perhaps a family together. They had been living at home with their parents and now feel ready to take this step into independent adulthood.

After six months of living together, they find that their relationship has somehow shifted. They fall into the common pattern of getting up each morning, going to work, then coming home, tending to some chores, unwinding, and having a few hours together. On their weekends, they may plan to see some friends or have the weekend away together. Over time, they both fall into these patterns and start to feel the relationship has lost its shine. The joyful excitement is replaced with repetitiveness and all the not-so-romantic day-to-day joys of living in close quarters with someone other than who you grew up with. Over time, there are the inevitable arguments, clashes in desires, or ways they believe things "should be done"— things that were not overly present in their two-year courtship when they didn't spend hours and days on end under the same roof.

As their arguments increase, their adoration of each other decreases. They start to "fall out of love" and no longer feel as they used to towards one another. After a time, as they drift apart, they decide to separate. They have little choice but to move back to their parents as they both individually consider the next steps in life.

Back with their parents, they are both going through the typical misery one does when having to adjust to the loss of someone they once loved. It starts to dawn on them how much they miss one another. The once annoying habits of their partner are now viewed with affection; they long to hear their partner's nuanced complaint about their morning coffee or some other such trivial exchange. They look at their bed and smile as they remember how their partner would always adjust the way the pillows were placed, which once might have led them to complain about it. This positive reminiscing and general missing of their partner carries on, and inevitably, one reaches out to the other, and they are in contact again. These feelings of loss and the hope and desire to be happy lead them to reconcile. They recommit to one another, and the relationship continues. They move back in together, the wedding is back on, and they both try to do better than before.

In an alternate world, they do not get back together, and one or both decide to start dating again. One has a string of bad relationships with no prospects of things improving, whereas the other eventually finds someone to settle down with. This new, functioning relationship could be more harmonious and fulfilling than the initial one, or it could be a shadow of what they had with their prior partner. In any case, they choose to make that relationship work. They don't want to go through the pain of another failed relationship and choose to make the most of what they have. The partner who didn't manage to find another relationship always considers what could have been. Perhaps this makes them bitter in some way, or perhaps they accept their losses. There is no accounting for how life will pan out for either of them. In fact, any outcome is possible.

So, what is the object of exploring the above possibilities? Well, hindsight is something that will often "show us the cost" and can lead us to try and repair a poor decision or at least prevent us from repeating it. However, this comes with pain or loss of having made that poor decision. Let's take a look at two points in this story where knowing the costs could have interceded the decision-making process and averted the breakdown of this relationship.

Moment 1: Moving in Together

This is the point at which their relationship faces the first big challenge. In the above scenario, we have two happy, "in love" 25-year-olds who are excited about their lives together. This is a beautiful thing, to be sure; however, because "love" is guiding their decision-making, and more importantly, it is likely clouding their ability to consider all the factors of their decision.

I use quotation marks around the word love for a reason, as "love" in this case is based on how the two of them see, understand, or feel it to be. At this stage, they may see or feel love as exciting, happy, and personally fulfilling. It is likely something they feel in the moment rather than understand across the next 50-plus years together. This is not a criticism of the couple but simply an observation of how many relationships progress. It's also not to suggest this is "bad," per se. However normal and expected this perception of love is, it is also a failure to know the cost at this crucial moment. Although I would argue that this view of love is beautiful and in many ways necessary (perhaps even correct in its design), it can leave people blindsided to the realities of what's to come and can prevent them from considering, let alone knowing, the cost of moving in together. They have not considered the cost of that love.

Until now, they had been able to spend only the "better" parts of their day together, which helped them avoid the mundane or strained parts of life. Moving in together would change this dynamic. If they understood how this change would occur, they could prepare for it, expect it, and even embrace it. They should be aware that moving in together means (costs) learning to tolerate aspects of their partner they might dislike, growing personally to maintain the relationship, and realizing that what seems quirky today might become frustrating tomorrow. The more aware we are of these costs, the more predictable the outcomes become.

Had they considered that moving in would change their dynamic, they would have to develop their love into a more mature love, one of respect, acceptance, and, importantly, dedication to the other. Then, they would likely be better prepared for what was to come. They would have entered this new stage knowing what was ahead and having already committed to accepting such things into their lives and their relationship. In essence, they must understand and prepare for the unpleasant costs as much as the pleasant gains.

To paint a poor analogy, when you buy a new car, let's say the car of your dreams, you expect it to run without issues. It's new, and you loved it well before it was yours. However, should it start to have issues, you start to resent it because it's not what was expected or promised. You didn't account for the cost of time and money for it to do what was promised. You fall out of love with this car, start to think you made a bad decision, focus on what's wrong with it, and forget all the reasons you fell in love with it. To further butcher this analogy, had you not expected it to be perfect from the start, had you expected it would need some work, or that you might need to learn how to maintain it, then the "issues" would likely be more tolerable. You would see them as quirks that you can grow to accept and love as they are part of the package. Had you been insightful enough to expect such "issues," or better yet, realize all cars come with one issue or another, then your expectations would have been more reasonable, and you would be more aware of the cost of that purchase, just as you would be more aware of the costs of moving in with your partner. Furthermore, during these times of frustration, should you be able to focus on what you do "love" about that car as a whole rather than focus on the issue it presents in the moment, then you would be more likely to accept, appreciate and value the fact that you have it.

Do not mistake this identification of normal issues or imperfections in relationships for a negative perception of relationships. In fact, I believe that if we can come to view a partner as a unique and intricate human being, one that comes with their own variations and perspectives on life, we can come to appreciate each other all the more. I view this as one of the amazing things about humanity, a true gift to really know another human and to be known by them. I would argue that seeing your partner's imperfections and accepting them as part of the package is what separates them from everyone else; it's what helps you realize you really do have a one-of-a-kind human being with whom you get to share a life. However, often, this requires adaptation on our own part. It requires that we ourselves grow and develop to be able to appreciate these things. The key is to be aware that this is one of the costs. Reality will fall short of your dreams and expectations well before it presents you with something you could never have dreamt of or expected.

Moment 2: The Breakup
The second key moment is their decision to break up. I've purposely given little detail as to why they broke up other than to say they were having some disagreements. This is by design, as I guess anyone who reads this and has had a breakup will likely project their own personal reasons for the breakup of their relationship.

Regardless of whether or not they reconcile, the point of breaking up is often a point of high or confusing emotions, and often, we do not consider the costs of this decision. We tend to act based on some degree of dissatisfaction or perhaps hurt felt by our partner's behavior or words. The negative experience, or perhaps lack of positive experience, tends to dominate and drive our decision or desire to separate. We focus on the negative aspect of something rather than the positive we once focused on. The more we focus on a negative aspect, the larger it grows in our minds, becoming an ongoing internal advertising campaign. As we repeatedly think about it, we become increasingly convinced that it's something we dislike and, therefore, view it as a problem. Gone are the days of focusing on the dreamy side of things, which often filled us with a desire to see or be with our partner.

So, what costs did they fail to consider? Again, all the ones that become obvious with hindsight. They fail to consider the emotional costs of losing the connection they had for over two years. Their focus on wanting relief from some issue has overpowered their focus on the human being they loved for two years and chose to live with. They fail to consider the impact this breakup might have on them going into future relationships, and perhaps this will become an unhelpful yardstick for comparing future relationships. Or, deeper yet, this decision to break up might start to teach the individual that when things get hard, leaving is always an option. Over time, this could develop the individual into a very unhelpful and unattractive personality of entitlement or expectation that someone will "fit them" as opposed to them having to develop in order to mutually "fit" with someone.

Their fixation on a disagreement may have blinded them to the fact that every relationship will have disagreements and that these disagreements are a common cost in any relationship. They failed to realize that focusing on the problem prevents them from focusing on the solution. They didn't consider that the cost of winning an argument means their partner loses one, which can harm the relationship. Additionally, they overlooked that focusing solely on what they want, rather than embracing the potential for growth and maturity that comes from going without, can be detrimental. They failed to realize that growth and hardship often lead to long-term fulfillment and happiness. By losing sight of this in their pursuit of "feeling good" or a constant feeling of love, they may inadvertently rob themselves of their own happiness.

The difficulty in knowing the costs of any decision is that of identifying the negative space, that is, the space or things that we are not looking at or are not aware of. Chances are that had this couple talked to their parents, grandparents, or even a professional about relationships, about what to expect, what might go wrong, and how to handle it, then they would be more aware of potential costs to the relationship and themselves. Of course, this assumes that what they hear is helpful or even predictive of what is to come for their specific relationship. The idea here is that the more wisdom or insight people have, the more likely they are to anticipate future challenges and assess their ability to handle them. In this context, insight can pertain to understanding both relationships and one's own personal tendencies.

This example looked at the decisions a couple *did* make. Let's now look at an example of an individual and the decisions they *didn't* make.

Example 2: The Costs of Keeping a Relationship

In this example, we look at a person, perhaps in their 30s or 40s, who is living with their spouse and their three young children. For the purposes of this example, we could choose either the mother or the father because the principle could apply to either.

They have been together for 15 years, neither has any desire to divorce, and both are committed to raising their family, but one is constantly struggling on a personal level. Their self-esteem is poor, and they have slipped in and out of depression over the years, which has affected their ability to work and be present with their children and spouse. This places a strain on their partner because nothing the partner does seems to have any lasting effect. They recognize that this situation is causing stress for their partner, and they genuinely do not want this for them. They are also aware it prevents them from being the parent they want to be to their children.

The partner feels that all the issues stem from unresolved problems with their parents, who have always been and continue to be negative, disapproving, and even abusive. They believe that maintaining contact with the parents perpetuates these issues. The person themselves recognizes the difficulties in their relationship with their parents, but due to a lifetime of seeking—and never receiving— acceptance, they cannot let go of the desire to prove their worth to them. They include their parents in their lives, inviting them to significant events like their wedding, housewarming, the birth of their kids, birthdays, and other family events, hoping to demonstrate their accomplishments and seek validation, acceptance, or praise. However, this acknowledgment never comes. Their partner sees this and believes it to be the root cause of their issues, impacting the entire family. Despite this, the person continues to believe things will get better, not realizing the damage it's causing to their home.

Each day, they unconsciously choose to seek their parent's approval, and their actions play this out despite repeated disappointments. They choose to continue the same course of action out of hope for a different and more favorable outcome without understanding the true costs it has on their spouse, their children, and themselves. They cannot see that their spouse is missing out on a much more fulfilling and happy relationship. Their decision to maintain their parents in their lives has already cost them 15 years of stress and reduced happiness. They are not aware it is costing their children access to a healthy, happy parental figure. In fact, should the children be exposed to seeing their parent being disparaged or abused by their grandparent, the child may be forming unhealthy views of the parent themselves. It is quite possible that this person's decision to keep the status quo, or indecision to make a change, is not only costing them their mental health but is also inadvertently shaping the mental health of their children and partner.

From an objective standpoint, the obvious solution here is to accept that they will never have the acceptance of their parents and learn to let go of this or choose to separate themselves from their parents entirely. The partner has likely suggested such a thing over the years, but for the person themselves, the strength required to give up something they have always wanted or needed is greater than they can muster. Sadly, it may take the breakdown of the family before this person really starts to see the cost of their "inaction." Perhaps it is when the partner finally walks out on them or when the children start presenting with issues of their own, such as depression, anxiety, or worse, that they realize the costs. These are scenarios that present themselves in the therapy room. On many occasions, I am faced with a tortured parent/partner who is forever chasing the approval of a parent that will never come. They unknowingly sacrifice their entire lives seeking this approval. Other times, I am faced with an adolescent child who is suicidal or otherwise in complete emotional disarray due to an essentially incapacitated parent. Sadly, in such cases, even if the adolescent comes to realize the core of the issue, the troubled parent refuses to accept they are contributing, let alone causing, the demise of their child. Perhaps this would falsely suggest to them that their child is now also not accepting of them as a parent/person, which would only compound their already desperately empty sense of acceptance.

Had they known the cost of clinging to the idea of parental acceptance, they may have abandoned this hope decades earlier. They may have come to realize they have the acceptance of their spouse (arguably a more valuable acceptance given it comes from a non-blood relative and chosen life partner) and of their children who only want to spend time with them and have shared experiences together. But as is the theme, when we focus too greatly on one thing, we tend to miss the others. We are blinded by our desires or strong emotions rather than being able to step back and take on the perspective of the dynamics that are affecting our lives.

Keep it simple: Emotions can often blind us to knowing the costs of our actions or inaction.

It can be easy to "know the cost" when reading examples such as these. As we look at someone else's circumstance, we have a certain emotional distance from it; the parts are clear to us, and so the solutions are also easier to come by. But it is this emotional detachment that allows us to rationally and logically consider things. Of course, having more insight into human nature, or generally having more life experience, helps with identifying possible solutions, but when we are emotionally tied to something, things are always hazier. We are all subject to blind spots, and often, these are tied to our emotional needs or reactions. Perhaps the old adage of "hindsight is 20-20" is a representation of not only learning from a mistake but also that the separation it gives us from emotion helps us to see things more clearly.

Conscious Decision-making

In the above examples, we not only see that there is a lack of consideration of the broader impacts of one's decisions but also that there are emotions and/or unconscious drivers that are silently impairing one's ability to do so. While the ability to know the cost of decisions is an intellectual exercise, it is often impaired or obscured by an emotional or unconscious process. In fact, when we are free of any emotional pull or unconscious drive, we are likely to be best at identifying the costs of some action. Often, this is why we consult with an independent party when we are trying to get a clear perspective on things. We know their emotional distance from the issue gives them a different, if not clearer, perspective. If we can be aware of any underlying influences of our own, then we can improve our ability to identify the costs we might be facing.

The Takeaway

No matter how beneficial the final outcome is, all actions or decisions have an associated cost or sacrifice. As they say, "Nothing in life is free." This is not to say that all costs are negative; simply, they are inevitable and need to be considered thoroughly. Consider the gain and the cost of any decision, especially if you are emotionally tied to the decision. Ultimately, if we want to limit unexpected outcomes that stem from our actions, we should stop to consider what any action could cost us. We only need to move forward with the action for which we are willing to pay the cost.

Chapter 8 – Factor 4: The Take-home Message

It's been argued that we are the sum of our memories and, therefore, the sum of our experiences. If this is true, then it would also hold that it is the sum of *how* we remember our experiences or how we encode and recall them that makes us who we are.

Encoding Our Take-home Message

Some might say that we simply remember things as they happened, but this is often not the case. Our perspective of what has happened in any scenario is often biased by earlier experiences or teachings. How we remember things will vary and is mediated by a number of factors, including personality, past experience, and even things such as culture, religion, and expectation. Most of us already realize this to be true, but for those who do not, feel free to ask a friend about an experience you shared years ago but have not spoken about since. See how similar your recollections are. Or better yet, go back to an old place such as a primary school, a kindergarten, or an old park you visited as a child. See how accurate your memory of that place is. You will likely find some differences between the reality of an event or place and your recollection of it.

In the case of an old school or park, your brain remembers that location from the perspective of being a child. It is likely biased by the fact that everything was bigger to you back then; you also had far less experience with emotions. Perhaps that park was the greatest place on earth when you were six, so your brain remembers it as such. At the time, it was the best place on earth, but now, with your expanded experiences and deeper understanding of emotion, your views change. With any luck, that park is no longer the best place on earth for you.

But what of the case of an old memory of being out with friends as an adult? You may have a different recollection from your friend due to other factors. Perhaps your recollection of that night out was negative, while your friend's recollection was positive. This could be due to your, or their, state of mind that day; perhaps you were stressed, or you misread the look you were given by someone that night. So, our state of mind will apply an unconscious bias to how we encode or recall things in general.

Internal Influence on Encoding

We all have internal worlds, with some of us being more susceptible to bias than others. Reasons for this can range from our genetic makeup to our early childhood influences. If a person is preoccupied with personal matters or obsessed with a particular belief, then they are more likely to express some sort of bias than a person that has a more objective or agenda-free perspective, hence why we seek independent third parties in dispute resolution.

To put the above into context, we could compare a bitter, angry, or vengeful person to a well-balanced, fulfilled, and grounded individual. Odds are that the latter will be *more likely* to observe things with less bias. This is not because the second person is any "better" or smarter than the first, but simply because their emotions are less likely to cloud their observation and encoding of events. Our emotions and beliefs have a strong impact on how we encode memories and what parts we tend to focus on.

This is not to say that the stereotypical "sage" will have a better "take-home message" than someone more emotionally driven. The reality is unless the observer has experienced and truly understood all aspects of human nature, they are unlikely to have a perfect perspective of any observation and, therefore, encoding of the event. At times, that "sage" who has lived a relatively privileged life alongside other well-adjusted individuals is more susceptible to being deceived by a lifelong sociopathic manipulator, for the sage is simply not experienced with such people and may not see it coming.

It is our take-home messages that combine to form our understanding of the world and ourselves in that world. Day after day, year after year, we encode what we experience in the world, and we do so based on what we encoded prior to that. The combination of these encoded memories will work to influence our personalities and impact how we interact with our world. This interaction then further influences what we experience and how that is encoded. Encode a series of negative, aggressive, or hateful experiences, and you are likely to view the world that way and then act accordingly. This does not mean that the world is negative, aggressive, or hateful, but it is to say that is how it was observed, which ultimately led to that person becoming more likely to be that way in response. The inverse is also true; some people will see the good in everything and feel that the world is good and, therefore, more likely to put that out into the world via their own interactions.

What matters here is what one sees and *how* they choose to encode it. This choice around how to encode can be something one actively works on. How easily it is achieved will often depend on how strongly they hold their current or preexisting beliefs, as well as how flexible they are with their thinking.

Keep it simple: How we encode our memories will be impacted by our moods, beliefs, and personalities, and each of these things is impacted by things we have encoded/experienced before. Our environment and the people in it sculpt us, and it is up to us to be mindful of what we allow to do this sculpting.

Take, for example, a scenario where a husband pays his partner a compliment. From the point of view of an external observer, this is largely seen as a positive or kind thing. However, how impactful or positive we see it will vary from person to person. There is likely to be a difference in how this is observed between a woman in her 70s with a history of poor relationships and decades without a kind word compared to a woman in her 40s with a loving husband who pays her compliments regularly. We could assume the 70-year-old may respond with some degree of sadness as she views something she lacks and longs for in life, while the 40-year-old woman may just see a typical couple with little emotional response at all.

The differing life experiences of these two female observers have an impact on what they see or how they interpret the events. They see the same thing; however, the emotional response or gravity of the situation may be different between them. The external experience is the same; the internal encoding of that experience may not be. That is, of course, if they allow themselves to passively encode the experience. Should they be more mindful and active in their mental encoding of the experience, they could potentially shift or amplify the emotional content of this observation. By doing this, they are exercising some influence over how they encode things and how their worldviews are sculpted.

Keep it simple: Our past experiences can influence current experiences. Challenging our passive assumptions or views can help us regain more control of how we develop moving forward.

We can further influence how we encode things by considering the potential back story to anything we may experience. In the case above, we could assume that the husband in the story has always struggled to pay compliments, perhaps because he never got any of his own and finds it hard to express such things. Perhaps his difficulty in expressing himself has put a strain on the relationship over many years and reduced the self-worth and happiness of his partner. By considering this, perhaps we will start to see his actions as even more meaningful. We start to interpret events slightly differently, and now we can encode that seemingly mundane event even more positively than before. The encoding may go along the lines of: "Oh, that's so nice. He went through so many struggles and realized he wasn't giving her all she deserved. Now he has lifted his game, got over his own internal world enough to really value her and their relationship, and is paying her the compliments she deserves!"

Of course, we have no way of knowing how accurate the above backstory is. It may be entirely inaccurate. Regardless, your take-home message will be more positive if viewed this way, or at the very least, it will be *changed*. That is the true point to illustrate here. We can change our experience and memory of something if we have more, less, or different information about it. One might say that making up a fake backstory in order to have a positive view is hardly a helpful or honest approach to life. This may be true but consider how many times a person's imagination or bias has created an inaccurate negative backstory or *assumption* about an experience and how unhelpful that has been.

By actively creating a backstory or challenging your instinctual perspective of an experience, we can sculpt how we encode something in our memory. Equally, we could just try to clear our minds of its bias. Without creating any backstory, we could pause, observe, and take in what we are seeing: a man who is showing kindness to a woman or two human beings sharing a human emotion and expressing that without care of how others view it. It is a display of love or, at the very least, kindness.

If we allow our default approach of encoding memories to continue, then so too will our current state. Our view of the world and ourselves is less likely to change if we allow our default, passive encoding to continue. If we want to shift our mindset, then we need to do so by either actively expanding on what we are seeing or removing the default filter by clearing away our bias from our observation.

Short of interrupting the couple to learn the backstory of their relationship, we will never know the true significance of what we have seen. We will only ever have our interpretation of the event. The question becomes how we choose to see such day-to-day events. This leads to the deeper question of whether we are aware of our unconscious training or bias. Do we know how it was formed? Importantly, do we realize how it is influencing our "take-home message" for everything we experience?

Directing Your Own Mindset

To be blunt, a person with depression is likely to view things in a disproportionately negative way. In the case of the example above, they are more likely to unknowingly create a negative backstory. Perhaps they would view the male as manipulative rather than kind or personalize things and think, "Everyone has someone except me!" Ultimately, they will unintentionally view things more negatively than they actually are, which will perpetuate their low mood. This becomes an automatic, unconscious negative bias, which is likely driven by previous negative experiences of their own and a core factor of a depressed state of mind.

In the case above, the person with depression, accurately or not, will have the take-home message that either nothing remarkable happened, or the male is manipulating their partner for their own gains. In any case, the take-home message is, at best, a neutral one, but more likely a negative one. This serves to perpetuate their current belief structure, which deepens their belief or bias towards things.

This biased process that we see in depression also plays out in every other mindset. A happy person determined to have a good time will innately apply a positive bias, a person fixated on money will view things through the lens of cost or profit, and someone who is preoccupied with romantic relationships will skew their worldview towards that in some way. Being aware of how we are influencing our own experience of things, and then how we are encoding them, gives us the ability to change or challenge this and start to sculpt our mindset towards where we want it to be rather than entrenching it deeper into where it is.

Keep it simple: Only when a person detaches from their bias can they see things from a new perspective.

On its own, how someone encodes this one event is unlikely to change their lives. But imagine all the years or decades of memories we have. Each one was encoded based on factors such as how we felt that day, what we were told by someone else, who we were with, how old we were, and perhaps what we wanted to believe at the time. If all these memories were encoded passively, then it is likely that our development into adulthood has been left in the hands of some default programming from our childhood. However, should we be more active and challenge our take-home messages, and how we choose to see things and encode them, then we can start to overcome our past biases or filters and direct our own views of the world and ourselves.

Keep it simple: Passively observing our world and encoding our experiences into memories runs a greater risk of perpetuating our "old ways." Taking a more active and mindful approach to choosing how to remember things allows us to have a greater influence in sculpting our mindset.

The power of a backstory is not to be underestimated. It can be a very strong way to influence your experience and memory of something. It is a technique that marketing and propagandists alike have used for decades, if not centuries. You'll see this when someone is given a backstory in a reality TV show to strengthen the audience's emotional attachment. Similarly, political narratives may paint a leader as evil to justify actions like going to war. The accuracy or truthfulness of these backstories is irrelevant to those creating them; only the outcome of how the population thinks and remembers things matters. As long as the masses are passive in their observation and encoding, then their minds are ripe for manipulation. However, should the masses be more active, more reflective, and considered of their observations prior to encoding, then they are in charge of their own minds and, ultimately, the development of their worlds.

Is All Bias Unhelpful?

It is important to highlight the difference between accurate and helpful bias when it comes to encoding. Let's take someone who has an innately positive bias on everything. They will encode everything with a positive skew, which, strictly speaking, is inaccurate. This positive bias no doubt helps to keep the individual positive and helps them maintain a state of happiness throughout their life, which can be argued is a good strategy. However, in the long term, this same person runs the risk of being out of touch with reality. If the reality is that of a declining environment or increasing poverty, then this positive person may not just struggle to accept this but will resist doing so. Should they be able to maintain their positive worldview in a declining world, they may be happier than others, but they would not be in touch with reality and may be detached from those around them, much as a depressed person is often detached from those around them.

Encoding inaccurately due to a positive bias is likely to result in a happier mood, at the risk of living in a "fantasy land" compared to those around them. Although this may not be an *accurate* representation of reality, it may still be best for that person as it keeps them in a better mood overall. Others may well argue that this person holds a delusional perspective and does nothing to motivate themselves or others towards improving reality (as they remain content in their belief that everything is fine). Realistically, they are holding an unrealistic view of the world, and should things take a turn for the worse, they are at greater risk of not adjusting to this, as well as giving out unrealistic advice to those around them. This is a trade-off between positivity and reality, not unlike the trade-off between negativity and reality in the case of depression.

Keep it simple: Biased encoding can be helpful or, at least, protective at times. A positive bias can help to keep our moods positive, which maintains one's functioning. However, its potential drawback is that of an increasing lack of connection with reality. A negative bias, however, is likely to only damage one's mood as they inaccurately view things as more negative than they are. This not only damages their current mood state but also draws them further away from reality over time, which leads them to be out of touch.

If maintaining a positive or negative bias in your encoding is fundamentally problematic, does "accurate" encoding provide a better path? Arguably, yes. However, as is often the case, better does not mean easier. In order to have an accurate encoding, one must first overcome the internal and external factors that work against it. Assuming this is achieved, they are then faced with having to accept the often-harsh realities of life with as much conviction as the beautiful ones. Assuming one gets this far, there is then the matter of being one of the few that has. Although this more accurate view of things is helpful, or arguably "better," it is certainly not easier. Galileo comes to mind. His belief (worldview) that the earth was round, while certainly more accurate, was less biased by what he was taught as a child, no doubt. It was ultimately a difficult view to hold and, given the lack of others who held it, proved fatal. As much as having a more accurate perspective on yourself and the world is helpful, it can prove difficult when there are few others who share the same approach. It can become increasingly difficult to find those who share the same view as the masses retain a bias that keeps them "safer" but more oblivious to the realities of the world around them.

When someone reaches a level of awareness where they can challenge the biases ingrained in us, they might encounter reactions like, "You're such a pessimist," "You're so distrusting," "People aren't like that," or even, "You think you're so smart." These responses can lead to isolation or a reduction in social contact, which might cause people to unconsciously conform with their peers. Positive peers might discourage a realistic view of negative events, while trusting friends might discourage them from skepticism towards untrustworthy individuals. In order to maintain social connections, people may compromise their more accurate understanding of *the* world and the people in it in order to retain having people in *their* world.

CHAPTER 8 – FACTOR 4: THE TAKE-HOME MESSAGE

The upside of achieving the ability to accurately encode events is that it offers us a clear view of reality and of ourselves. This means we are in the best position to understand our world both independently of and inclusive of ourselves. We can accurately understand the reasons behind something without incorrectly applying blame to ourselves or others. We can view other people's actions for what they are and not personalize things needlessly. We can identify our own bias and take responsibility for it. We do not delude ourselves into thinking that things are better or worse than they are, and so we become better by identifying the costs of things. We see other people's agendas for what they are and are less likely to fall into the Primary Pitfall.

Note: I maintain that we are all prone to some degree of bias in our encoding. When I refer to those who can accurately encode, I mean instances of mostly accurate encoding rather than perfect accuracy at all times. At best, their encoding is mostly accurate most of the time. Additionally, I am referring to adults rather than children, as children, with their still-developing brains, cannot be expected to form an accurate, unbiased view of things.

Keep it simple: Accurate encoding provides a clear representation of reality, which puts us in the best position to then address and incorporate events into our lives and development. This accurate encoding is difficult to attain as we must combat internal and external influences such as personal bias, societal norms, and other people's agendas.

Ultimately, the entire purpose of wanting to remove one's bias from their encoding is to help them have a more accurate view of themselves and the world. By achieving this, we can start to understand more accurately who we are and how we fit into the world around us. It gives us a better perspective of our true abilities and limits, as well as letting us see others for who they truly are rather than through our own biased lens.

External Influences on Encoding

As stated earlier, there are any number of things that can influence how we see things. I mentioned culture and have alluded to time or age. Let's say we change the previous scenario slightly and then apply a different culture and time. Let's assume the couple we observed were two gay men. The location is still a supermarket, but this time, it is in 1940s Germany, or perhaps a strict Muslim nation under Sharia law. All of a sudden, we have to consider the cultural or political climate, what that society was presently teaching about such an exchange, what was permissible, what people were *expected* to say or do in such a scenario, and so on. How do we now encode or remember this? We could shift this again by retaining the gay couple but moving to San Francisco in 2020. A shift in time and/or culture, and suddenly, we see this scenario quite differently, as did the people of that time and place. Conceivably, it could be the same person who had observed this hypothetical gay couple in 1940 and 2020. How might their encoding of this be?

We like to think that we are in control of how we remember things and that we experience things for what they truly are. In truth, our observations are always influenced by internal (age, mood, bias) and external (culture, peer pressure, era) factors. Despite this, we are not always at the mercy of these factors to the point that we always encode things inaccurately. It is certainly possible, at least at times, to not be influenced or controlled by societal pressures. After all, not all citizens informed on those fleeing or hiding from the Nazi regime in 1940s Germany. It is also possible, albeit with a degree of effort, to be aware of one's own biases and account for them when encoding a memory. However, for the most part, people tend to encode on autopilot, meaning they unknowingly permit their environment and own personal feelings to skew their observations and memory encoding. No doubt you have seen a friend misread an event, or it has been pointed out to you that you are misreading or misremembering something. Equally, on a broader scale, we have seen populations of people behave in questionable or even reprehensible ways throughout history.

CHAPTER 8 – FACTOR 4: THE TAKE-HOME MESSAGE

Keep it simple: Do not underestimate the strong impacts of external factors on your encoding of memories, be it culture, media/advertising, traditions, politics, or historical norms.

I feel compelled to highlight the importance of being aware that our views and beliefs are always influenced by external pressures on both a subtle and insidious level. In fact, how we live our lives is very much dictated by these external forces, many of which we are not consciously aware of. This can be seen across history as cultures sway from one set of values to another, from family values to economic, political, or military. Take the United States as an example. Its transition of values as a country has shifted significantly over the past 100 years, and although there are individuals within that country who maintain consistent values over time, the nation as a whole influences its people's lifestyle based on the national agenda.

This concept can also be applied on a smaller scale, such as within a family unit or even an individual's development. Any given environment can pressure a person or family to adjust their expectations of behavior, thoughts, and what is deemed acceptable in a group or society. Consequently, how we encode experiences changes as well. For example, if an environment normalizes and promotes aggression, individuals living in that environment will encode aggression as positive or at least beneficial. Any harm resulting from that environment would be attributed to factors other than aggression, as aggression is perceived as good. Thus, they encode positive memories of that aggression unless they later find themselves in a different environment that emphasizes the negatives of aggression. In such an opposing environment, they might re-evaluate their encoding of those past events.

In essence, our environments, or societies, can very much sculpt our beliefs of what is acceptable and how we view ourselves within that environment. Even a smaller-scale environment, such as a school, can have this effect. A musician in a school that only promotes athleticism may have the challenge of how he views himself and how he encodes what he values compared to his peers and, therefore, the culture. An awareness of what our environment promotes is crucial to developing a healthy and more accurate encoding of events. The importance of highlighting these factors is not to demonize society or nations but to highlight that these factors play a significant part in our expectations of ourselves, which in turn sets the bar for our happiness. When our lives align with these expectations, we tend to feel satisfied or happy, and when we fall short, we feel failure and sadness.

What we see here is that how we encode things is also influenced by how we are expected to or how we are taught to. If we were to be taught as a culture that all human value is tied to one's financial gain and nothing else is of importance, then perhaps no one would pursue or consider things that are not financially profitable. Perhaps, if we are taught flattery is only useful if it progresses you financially, then we observe and encode that compliment in the supermarket as a business transaction. Furthermore, if we are not doing well financially in a culture that only values monetary gain, then we start to view ourselves as worthless and fall into a state of depression (despite being a musical or scientific genius). If we are expected to achieve something, in this case, wealth, then we are happy if we do and depressed if we do not. Ultimately, it is what we and our environment expect of us that sets the bar for what makes us happy.

Again, the objective here is to indicate how our brain encodes a given experience based on what belief it has been led to hold. One example of how our socially taught expectations influence our encoding of memory would be the case of the "failing success" story. This is the story of any person who, by today's standards, is living an average life in terms of wealth and social standing. This person may have a home to live in, a family, and meaningful work but is dissatisfied or even depressed. They have an average life by the standards of the time but feel dejected as they are not above average. Should this person have what they have now but lived 100 years earlier, they would be considered kings with their flushing toilets and magical air conditioning. They would likely see themselves as kings and feel significantly happier as they are well above average. In truth, however, they have nothing more than they did before we put them 100 years into the past. Their external world has changed their perspective on who they are or what they have, but in reality, they have the same house, family, and work.

This example is given to illustrate how external influences shape our belief structure. On some level, this person has encoded that they are a failure by virtue of their environment and not by virtue of who they are or what they have.

Now that we know internal and external factors can impact how we encode our experiences and how we remember events, the question arises of how this helps us in tackling things such as depression, anxiety, or just general life experiences.

The idea is that when you are more aware of your bias and the external pressures pushing and pulling on how you experience and remember things, you are able to resist or remove these factors that are preventing you from seeing things accurately and having a true understanding of reality. The depressed person will often find it extremely difficult not to view things negatively, including themselves. However, once they are aware that this is what they are doing, they are a step closer to changing this encoding. Add to this the understanding that their expectations of life and themselves have also been sculpted by an environment they just happened to be born into, and they can further challenge if that environment is one they agree with. Encoding for those with depression or anxiety is often very biased and unconscious in nature. Making this a more conscious and accurate process can shift their mindset and improve their well-being. I have found this is often a pivotal point in their recovery.

This same premise is applied to non-clinical cases. Becoming aware of how one's history is impacting their view on present matters can lead them to have a greater understanding and control of their thoughts and actions, which in turn will influence their feelings. Coming to such an awareness can often help a person process unresolved past issues. They can come to a state of self-forgiveness or an understanding they are not to blame. It can lead a person to not play out past relationship issues with new partners and be more conscious of how to raise their children rather than play out the faults of their own childhood.

The Importance of Early Encoding

How we encode things today will impact how we encode new things tomorrow. So, how we encode things from a young age will impact our lifelong trajectory. Children are not aware of their internal biases nor any external influence, at least not consciously. This is perhaps why a parent might say something like, "You don't mean that. You're just angry right now." With guidance such as this, the parent plays a role in helping the child encode their experience, as does the child's broader community. As adults, our awareness of internal and external factors helps us to ensure a more accurate and helpful encoding of reality. This, however, is not easy, even for an adult, and often takes a concerted effort. One would need exceptional insight and awareness of their thought processes and tendencies, as well as an intricate analysis and understanding of their environment. It is also difficult to isolate how much of our internal process is purely *us* and how much is influenced by our environment throughout our development. With all these difficulties, is it any wonder why most people run on autopilot or seek extensive psychotherapy to better understand their inner workings?

Any therapist will be abundantly aware of how a person's upbringing and general life experience impact their view of the world and themselves. It's the reason a therapist takes a life history with a focus on early and pivotal life experiences. Although the client is aware of their childhood experiences, they lack other points of comparison to understand how their development might have been different under alternate circumstances. Could we really know how a traumatized person would develop had they not been traumatized? It might be fair to say they would suffer less, but would anything else about that person be different? Would they be more trusting? Kinder? Less compassionate to others? Any number of factors could be different, and although we could make some safe assumptions about them being less pained in life, we cannot accurately know in what other ways they would be different as a person. We can only look at providing such a person with retrospective therapy or insight into events, with the hope that this leads them to re-encode events to create a better, healthier perspective and, ideally, live a better or easier life moving forward. While they may achieve recovery, their personality and neurology are less likely to change significantly. They are likely to retain certain traits due to early trauma, traits others wouldn't have without a similar history. Although the re-encoding can be helpful, it can't erase their past or allow them to live a trauma-free childhood.

Let's explore and illustrate this concept with the following example. A child born into a certain religious doctrine is likely to grow up believing in that religion and following whatever teachings are associated with it. They are more likely to view outsiders as "sinners" or "heathens" and view the world as being largely full of "lost souls" or some other such term. They will form memories of being a minority and may feel isolated, different, or compelled to convert or educate the masses. They have been taught that they are right and the masses are wrong, and so, when they talk with others that are not of their religion, their take-home message will be that much of the world is lost or on the wrong path. They are taught that they have to help these people in some way, or perhaps separate from them, so as to not be negatively impacted by them. Their worldview changes vastly due to their belief structure. Their take-home message or encoding of memories is very much biased by this religious influence.

Had this child been born to different parents, perhaps even the parents living next door, they would not have viewed the world through this good/evil lens and they would have seen the very same world in a very different way. They would encode their experiences of the world very differently. The so-called lost souls are now seen as regular people. The non-churchgoer is no longer a "lost soul" but just a typical person.

The foul-mouthed, verbally abusive drug addict is not seen as a sinner but as someone who is unpleasant to be around. In fact, absent of a strong environmental force such as religion in this example, the person would more likely be influenced by the broader, popular culture and be far more like everyone else; they would likely be one of the masses. None of this is to say that one is "better" than the other. After all, community influence can be good or bad, just as religious influence can be.

How we are taught to encode, remember, or view things places a different lens between us and the world. Some lenses are more helpful or clearer than others. Some are harmful, and some are just slightly different hues but provide a similar picture. Importantly, none of us choose what lens to look through as children, and out of habit, many do not choose to examine what lens they look through as adults.

Regardless of what lens was provided to you, its effects are very important, for while that lens is in place, you are encoding or developing a worldview and a view of yourself within that world. In other words, it is sculpting who you are and how you see reality. The person brought up in a religion is likely to hold that religion's views for the rest of their life. At some point, they may leave that religion, but their mind is forever aware of the perspective that religion takes, and there will always be part of their brain that views things from that perspective should they choose to. They cannot *un-see* that perspective; they can only choose to continue to adopt it or not.

Equally, a child whose lens was provided by an abusive parent will also see the world differently and forever be aware of how bad and damaging people can be. The religious or traumatized child was not born religious or traumatized; it was not genetics that made them that way, nor was it them choosing these environments and developmental trajectories. We cannot say that the true nature of that child is religious or traumatized. These are just things that were forced upon them, lenses that were placed between the world and their brain, forcing them to see and encode the world a certain way.

This is the case of a child becoming who they are because of their environment, or more accurately, their genetic or core self, responding to the environment they were placed in. Should it be possible to go back and relive life, and we were to place that same child in an environment free of trauma or religion (or perhaps a different religion), then we would almost certainly see this person develop differently. What was a Christian child might now be a Muslim child. What was a frightened, avoidant child might now be a confident, active child. This is not to suggest they become an *entirely* different person, as some traits would remain, but there is no doubt that the person would have a different beginning, which places them on a different developmental trajectory.

What we are exploring in this example is how external factors can sculpt how a person encodes memories and what beliefs or views develop. These memories and beliefs go on to shape future biases or world views, which further form who that person becomes. Of course, what lenses they adopt in adolescence and adulthood will also sculpt their development. Should they remain passive about their childhood lens, then they are likely to follow in that same vein. Should they be more active and conscious of their choices, then they will start to have more control or influence over what lenses they choose and how they develop as a person.

This is why it can be difficult to determine if it is wholly and solely *us* that is biasing our take-home message or if it is something that was in us by an external factor throughout our lives. It could be argued that ultimately, the external sources of influence sculpt the internal, and so we are all just a representation of our environment. However, that would suggest that we have no power at all over who we are or who we become, and there are many who take the time to engage in self-examination and "change their ways" by challenging their currently held beliefs.

Perhaps the differentiation of what is *us* (internal) and what has sculpted us (external) is not critical in understanding the importance of "the take-home message." What is critical is the understanding that how we *choose* to remember something will shape and impact who we become in the future. As children, we do not have much of a choice as our brains are simply not capable of this. However, as adults, we do have a choice in how we view things, regardless of how hard or impossible it may seem.

There are countless stories of those who have lived objectively horrible lives, such as victims of trauma, abuse, poverty, ongoing neglect, and abandonment, who manage to turn their lives around from one of drugs and despair into one of happiness and success. These are the people who were able to adopt a new lens for their lives. They likely had help in doing so, but they are examples of how such a change is possible despite extreme circumstances. Unfortunately, not all are able to achieve this same sort of turnaround; any number of factors may not have aligned for them to do so. On a more widely relatable level, there are those who continue to have negative or undesired patterns in their lives, mostly due to not being able to change the lens they see and operate through.

Keep it simple: As children, we are all victims of our upbringing, and the lens that we view ourselves and the world through is very much provided to us. As adults, we have the option to change this lens should we choose to. What lens we choose will affect how we see the world and ourselves, and each day we encode through a given lens, it impacts our inner world, our beliefs, and hence our attitudes and behaviors going forward.

What We Forgot to Encode

Another important factor in encoding is what we felt was important to encode versus what we did not realize we could encode. This is essentially the case of focusing on the wrong lesson or on one piece of information and neglecting another.

Often, I will sit with a client and hear a series of events that have significant meaning and impact on their lives. They recount the event with great accuracy and perhaps provide more information than they realize; however, their focus is on only one element of the story. This one element is understandably the one that has stuck in their mind; it is what they took from the experience and focused on. Perhaps it was the most obvious element of the story, the one with the strongest emotional impact, or the one that they see repeated the most often in their lives. It is understandable that this element is their focus. Unfortunately, it's not always the most important element of the story, or its meaning entirely changes once they consider or identify other elements. Usually, when identifying and combining a few key elements, they can start to have a clearer, broader, and healthier perspective.

As always, let's explore this with some examples. Imagine a school-age child, 10 or 15 years old, male or female, who finishes second in a competition of their choice. They come home feeling despondent because they did not win. Perhaps this competition was their passion, and they spent all year or many years practicing with hopes of winning and achieving greater things. They focus on the fact that they came second, that they are not the best, and that things did not go their way. This is a completely normal and understandable response for a child. Their focus on losing is neither strange nor difficult to understand.

However, any reasonable adult could point out numerous other things to focus on. They could tell the child that coming second means they beat dozens or hundreds of other children. They could highlight how much the child has improved from the previous year, the skills they have learned, and how this second place can motivate them to train harder. They could also simply express how proud they, and the rest of the family, are of the child's hard work and excellent performance.

Depending on the particulars of the competition and the child's journey up until that point, there could be any number of other areas to focus on, none of which change the second placing or the disappointment of that. They could, however, show other equally or perhaps more meaningful learnings from the experience. The take-home message could be that they improved or beat 99% of their peers rather than they fell short of first place. What they choose to focus on or what they choose to encode from the event will make a difference for them going forward. At that key point of finishing second, they are unknowingly choosing to encode disappointment or encouragement; they are setting the path for inferiority or confidence. Which of these bricks they lay for their path in life will depend on their prior bias (or teachings) and whether or not someone steers them otherwise.

People who cannot find other important elements to focus on often fall back on their default biases, resulting in only a superficial or prescribed understanding of their circumstances, themselves, and the world at large. Being aware of what we are focusing on and being able to expand this focus to other aspects is a key skill for taking control of our personal development. Knowing what to focus on, how long to focus on it, and how to encode it with a broader perspective is critically important.

This is a relatively straightforward and surface-layer example. But what if we consider a more emotionally charged situation? Let's consider loss, a common issue that often arises in a therapeutic setting. It could be any loss, but let's take the example of a client coming to therapy after the death of a loved one. Understandably, the client is in a state of grief, sadness, and perhaps anger; in any case, they are distressed and struggling to cope with the loss. Their focal point is also understandably the loss of that person and what this means for their life. Sadness and depression can often result as they are powerless to resolve the issue—they cannot bring the person back. They continue to focus on what is missing.

All of this is reasonable. The client is certainly not wrong in their understanding of the situation, and emotionally and rationally, they are viewing the loss *accurately*. However, it is what they are not focusing on that is keeping them in their state of loss and despair. Of course, focusing on no longer having that person in their life will create sadness. However, what they have not focused on is what might help them overcome their state more easily, not because they are wrong in feeling their loss, but because that is not the path to recovering from it. Should they start to consider other factors to focus on, they could start to incorporate a broader perspective and have the opportunity to be impacted by factors other than the obvious loss.

In this case, understanding that feelings of loss indicate the value and importance of the person in their lives can be crucial. This reflection can lead them to appreciate how fortunate they were to have had such a person at all. They can consider what this person brought into their lives and what remains despite the loss. By recalling shared moments, they can form a greater appreciation for having had this person in their lives. They can also reflect on how the loved one shaped them and influenced their memories and actions, focusing on the positive impacts rather than the physical loss. Considering how their lives might have been without knowing this person can also foster gratitude.

This perspective does not remove the pain and loss but highlights that the intensity of their feelings reflects something of great value in their lives. Although the loved one is physically gone, their experiences, lessons, and influences remain. They will feel this loss for the rest of their lives; it is about how they integrate this feeling and let it shape them moving forward. Do they incorporate this experience and continue with life, or remain stuck in that negative moment, and for how long?

To be clear, a person needs to focus on what is not always helpful to understand and process it—in this case, the loss of a loved one. The unpleasant feelings are as valuable as the pleasant ones. In this example, the client may need to focus on the unpleasant feelings long enough to acknowledge and mourn their loss. However, there comes a time when dwelling on these feelings can become harmful or at least hinder their recovery.

People can often focus on one element of a situation to the exclusion of others. Allowing them to tell their story in their own time often leads them to consider other aspects of the story that could be focused on—elements that hold meaning and that they likely know about but have not yet considered.

Memory Encoding vs Internal Dialogue

We have discussed how innate biases can impact how we encode experiences. This innate bias acts as the lens through which we see things. We also highlighted the value of others guiding us through this bias to achieve a broader and more balanced perspective, allowing us to see the event in its entirety rather than encoding it passively in a potentially unhelpful way.

There is another key factor to consider: our internal dialogue. This is the voice in our heads that filters and comments on much of what we do or experience. It can be called inner dialogue, self-talk, or our thoughts, and some even believe it is their brain and, therefore, *themselves*. I simply refer to it as self-talk, and its influence on both our encoding and recollection is perhaps the most impactful element in the entire process, especially in adulthood. In childhood, this self-talk is arguably not yet fully formed and is not nearly as impactful as the voice of their parents.

Let's consider an uncomfortable example. Take any scenario where you have become embarrassed—it doesn't matter what the scenario is, just that it's embarrassing in some way. Chances are, when this scenario played out, you wanted to hide or escape. Even now, you probably don't want to think about it, and you certainly didn't want it to happen at the time. Chances are your internal dialogue had something to say about the scenario at the time. It may have been some commentary to run away, hide, or both. It may have doubled down and made you feel even worse. It may have been stuck in your mind for days, with thoughts like, "I can't believe I did that. I can never face them again." It may have led to you avoiding people or places or convinced you that you are the butt of all jokes. Or you may have been one of the lucky ones who were able to laugh it off; your internal dialogue was quick to realize these things happen to everyone, and laughing about it just like everyone else was the best strategy. In any case, what that internal dialogue says about the scenario will influence how you encode it. Do you still remember it as something shameful or embarrassing? Do you look back and think it was just something that happened, or are you able to laugh about it even when it's raised by someone who was there?

The embarrassment scenario is largely innocuous and makes little significant difference in someone's life in the long term. However, in a clinical setting, this internal dialogue process plays a very big role. A client (or perhaps yourself) may have a very negative mindset. Their take-home message is always one of not being liked, self-conscious, or, very commonly, not good enough. They attend a party and fail to make any friends, so they innately believe they are not liked. Their internal dialogue then doubles down, and for days or weeks on end, this message is drilled home with intensity. The person is convinced, by their own voice/thought, that they are not liked. They experienced this for days even though the party itself only lasted a few hours. Worse still, it is all based on their less than reliable assumption that no one likes them, simply because they didn't make a new friend at some party.

Keep it simple: How we choose to remember something will shape and impact who we become in the future.

Our internal dialogue helps us process events, make sense of them, and encode them into memory. If done accurately, it provides a reliable record of real-life experiences that can guide us in similar future scenarios. However, if done inaccurately, it creates biased memories that can be more harmful than helpful.

For example, being poorly treated in a relationship might lead someone to believe all men/women are bad, causing them to avoid future relationships or approach them with skepticism and negativity. This internal dialogue is not always objective, balanced, or well-informed. The emotional pain from a failed relationship can fuel misguided beliefs that all relationships are painful or doomed to fail.

This biased dialogue reacts to emotional pain rather than rationality, leading to mistakes and inaccuracies. It inaccurately generalizes specific events despite the fact that if all relationships were truly doomed, the idea of relationships would have been abandoned long ago.

Despite this, the person still tends to believe what their thoughts or inner dialogue says. After all, we all like to believe that what we think is right. None of us consciously chooses to be wrong about something. When we are unaware of our unconscious bias or an emotional defense structure being triggered, then we do not realize the error in our thinking. Our inner dialogue can very much be fueled by past failure and injury as it unconsciously acts to protect us and steers us away from something it thinks will cause pain or injury. The fact that it does this at the expense of other potential rewards, such as a successful relationship, is irrelevant at the time. The mind is focused on self-preservation. Of course, many people will "get over" the pain and hurt of a failed relationship and pursue another relationship in the future. Perhaps their desire for partnership eventually overrides the mental defense it had learned earlier, or perhaps some new insight comes to mind, and they re-encode things. This is a sign of flexibility and resilience, which are considered healthy traits. Those with a more rigid or brittle perspective are more likely to struggle and become *stuck* in their ways.

Keep it simple: Our internal dialogue plays a part in how we encode a memory. An accurately encoded memory can be a helpful template for the future, while an inaccurate encoding of memory can lead to future difficulty or a self-fulfilling prophecy.

Bringing it all Together

Following the idea discussed at the start of the book, our brain's primary purpose is to keep us alive, and we instinctively trust it. To complicate matters, most people see their brain as themselves, assuming their thoughts are their own. This leads to two issues:

1. We assume our brain is always telling the truth, which is why people stand by their beliefs, can be stubborn, and do not want to admit they are wrong.

CHAPTER 8 – FACTOR 4: THE TAKE-HOME MESSAGE

2. Since we identify with our brain, we rarely question it. This differs from how we treat the rest of our body. For example, if our arm or leg twitches involuntarily, we dismiss it as a strange error without assigning it meaning.

However, we don't apply this same logic to our brain. We fail to consider that a thought could just be a mental twitch or a reaction where the brain miscalculates. Instead, we believe that if the brain, or "I," thought something, it must have meaning. I argue that it often does not. A thought is just a thought—an option, not a fact or a decision—much like a movement is just a movement, not necessarily a dance or a deliberate choice.

The brain, like a muscle, develops through repeated actions. From birth, our internal dialogue forms from external influences—messages from others, beliefs, and environmental factors—all shaping our "self-talk." This dialogue, a mix of accurate and inaccurate messages, can be trained in various ways. By questioning its automatic processes, individuals can reality-check themselves. They gain the ability to choose what beliefs to reinforce rather than perpetuate existing ones. This active approach allows for new paths, steering away from past patterns towards self-directed growth.

Keep it simple: The take-home message, or what we tell ourselves in response to a life experience, will very much impact how we remember that experience and then shape how we behave in or view future experiences. This is no small thing; it is essentially influencing who we are going to become. Inaccurate encoding leads to a higher likelihood of difficulty down the road, so it's in our best interests to encode things accurately.

How do we go about accurate encoding? It can be easy to say, "Just remove your biases and observe things correctly," but how do we do this, and how do we know if we are being accurate even without a bias?

Honing the Take-home Message

Let's assume for a moment that we remove a person's biases and ask them to accurately observe some experience, such as two people at a restaurant or cafe. We could ask the observer to try to understand their interaction and, from that, determine the most accurate encoding or take-home message of that experience. They can consider how those people interact and whether it is normal for them. Is one having a bad or a good day? Is their lovely interaction typical? Or have they just come out of years of hard times, and this is the first day of a new chapter for them? Is the disagreement you are overhearing as conflictual as it sounds, or is that just their communication style? Perhaps their long stretches of silence are not due to them having little in common or being angry, or perhaps they have had a stressful or traumatic week, and being able to sit peacefully together in relative silence is a testament to their understanding of what the other needs or wants right now.

It does not take long before you realize that there are simply too many unknown factors behind the idea of "accurately observing" a situation. Even if we try to remove our personal bias so that we do not view things negatively or positively, there will likely be a lack of information to get a truly accurate observation. So, we will have to make some assumptions and likely introduce our own perspectives about what is happening, reintroducing a form of bias out of lack of information.

We can simply observe and state what we see as fact, and we can encode something without any assumptions or emotionality. We can just rationally encode that we saw two people talking in a cafe and draw no conclusions from the exchange. One could, for example, encode the following: "Two people, a couple, talking in a café, they were not talking much," or: "Two people in a café, who seemed to be a couple, were sharing a table." Importantly, in both cases, the person is not assuming anything beyond what anyone else would see. A smile is just a smile, and no depth of thought is offered. People were either nice or not nice to each other, and the reasons or meaning behind it is not entered into.

However, it also raises the question of whether they missed an opportunity to encode something meaningful. In some ways, we all choose *how* and *what* we are encoding. What matters is whether your encoding strategy is *helpful* or not. Perhaps, at times, choosing to encode things more positively, even when they were objectively neutral, is a good strategy. After all, it will lead to a more positive mindset in the future. However, if that positive mindset is too distant from the reality of the world, you may run the risk of being *out of touch*. Again, this is up to the individual to decide if that's the strategy they want to take.

Interestingly, this encoding is or can be a choice. Many of us will simply encode things based on our natural tendencies or biases. We encode automatically without conscious awareness of how our biases or past teachings affect our current encoding. Having worked with many clients who have had difficult, abusive, and neglectful upbringings, it is common to see their bias as one of negativity or low expectations. They do not actively "choose" to do this; it is an automatic response to their past teachings. When they become aware of this, they can start to catch their automatic bias and shift it. They can actually *choose* how to view things and start to have some agency over who they will become in the future.

A truly rewarding part of psychological work is when clients learn that although they cannot change their past, they can start to direct their future by directing their "self-talk" and choosing how to encode things. They learn they can impact their own take-home message and regain some control over their lives.

Keep it simple: What matters is what your take-home message is and knowing that if you are aware of your biases, you can choose to run with them or act against them. In any case, you have a choice over how you encode things, and you have some control over your take-home message.

When the Scenario Involves Us

The purpose of the above example of two people in a cafe was only to highlight that we can exercise choice over how we encode things. It is a scenario where we ourselves are not directly involved, and so it is easy to maintain a more rational perspective when making choices about what we saw or experienced. Because we are detached from the event, and it does not directly include us, it is easier to stay in that rational mindset and be aware of our assumptions. However, when the scenario directly involves us or is solely about us, this tends to change. We tend to slip into a more emotional, biased, or self-conscious mindset. This is expected as we are now having to not just observe something but also represent ourselves in a real-life experience.

When we're personally involved in an interaction, its outcomes hold greater significance. Our brains become more engaged, analyzing our actions and interpreting others' words and gestures. Questions like "Did I handle that well?" or "What did they mean by ____?" start to arise. These personal scenarios often trigger biases and can lead to encoding errors, influencing the beliefs we form about ourselves over time.

Here's a stereotypical example of a boy and a girl on a date. His take-home message is: "She didn't say a lot, so she didn't like me." In reality, she was too nervous or shy to be able to engage much and preferred to listen rather than talk. Should such a scenario play out a handful of times, the boy may very well start to make assumptions such as, "She didn't like me, girls don't like me, I'm not liked," and so on. This can then lead to low self-esteem, all because of an inaccurate assumption and "take-home message."

These two examples—one where we observe from outside the experience and one where we are directly involved—illustrate how perspective influences our thinking. When we are inside the experience, our thoughts can become more intense and subjective. More emotional, and less rational.

Another aspect of perspective involves enhancing our understanding of scenarios we're involved in. When trying to accurately interpret our interactions with others, having insight into their thoughts and feelings is crucial. For example, in a scenario like a "quiet first date," a man may assume a woman isn't interested in him if she seems reserved. However, if he understands common feelings and behaviors

CHAPTER 8 – FACTOR 4: THE TAKE-HOME MESSAGE

on a first date from her perspective, he can factor this into his thinking. Even better, he could take proactive steps to ease her shyness or anxiety, improving their interaction.

Alternatively, either person could address the quietness directly by asking if the other is nervous if they are typically reserved, or if something specific is on their mind. This approach helps both parties gain perspective on the situation, reducing the risk of misinterpretation or taking things personally.

If we try to take the perspective of the other person/people in our exchanges and consider from their point of view what *may* be happening, we can broaden our thinking, make it less about us (less personalization), and potentially get a more accurate perspective on the exchange. Of course, this depends on us accurately understanding things from the other person's perspective. If we know them very well, then we have a good chance of this, but if they are not known to us, this becomes more difficult as we have to rely on our general understanding of people. As we have seen earlier regarding the primary pitfall, this could lead to very poor outcomes, especially if we project too much of ourselves onto the other person.

A key element of reducing your risk of encoding an unhelpful and inaccurate take-home message is being able to consider events from the perspective of others and avoid your default personal mindset with your biases and self-doubts. Instead, try to observe the two people in a café and remove yourself from the situation.

Avoid jumping to conclusions, making assumptions, and, most of all, personalizing the situation based on your insecurities or unhelpful thinking strategies, no matter how loudly that inner dialogue is screaming at you. Realize that the importance of your exchange is no greater than that of the two strangers you saw in a cafe.

Do this if for no other reason than to calm your anxious/worried mind so you can better access your rational, objective self. Ask yourself what assumptions you are making like the boy did for the "quiet date." Identify these assumptions and make sure they do not get encoded as "fact" but as possibilities.

Encode the rational, objective information you do have, then set about finding more information about the things you objectively cannot be sure of yet. Do not encode things you are not sure of; leave them as "open cases" that have yet to be solved. Perhaps you solve them later that day or later that week when you speak to the person. Or perhaps it takes months or years to "close a case."

As much as we might like to close the case quickly, we should not do this at the expense of accuracy. Closing a case accurately months down the road is far more beneficial than closing a case inaccurately on the day. Remember, what we encode starts to become who we are.

If the boy on the quiet date encodes that the girl doesn't like him, he may be too fearful to call her again and miss out on a meaningful relationship. Worse still, if he encodes this same thing on subsequent dates with other girls, he ultimately encodes that he is unlovable, and all because he was in a hurry to encode, had a narrow perspective, or was too fearful to raise the question.

Keep it simple: Avoid encoding assumptions or personalizations.

Good Enough Encoding and How to Reduce Errors

I stated earlier that improving perspective is a way to reduce the risk of unhelpful encoding and that improving accuracy is also helpful in increasing your chances of a helpful take-home message. I say *improve* your chances, but I am not convinced there is a way of ensuring complete accuracy or how exactly we would measure such a thing. However, the accumulation of *better* encoding can only be beneficial for a person as they get a more accurate perception of themselves and others over time. Of course, some exchanges between people are straightforward, and having a complete understanding of that exchange is possible, but to have an entirely accurate understanding of oneself or others may be impossible and unnecessary.

CHAPTER 8 – FACTOR 4: THE TAKE-HOME MESSAGE

The objective of the take-home message is to have a good enough understanding to encode things that are as close to reality as possible. Often, our best tool in checking how close to reality we are is to ask a close, trusted friend about their view, then ask another and another. If all their perspectives align with yours, then that is a good sign that your internal influences are *not* impacting your perspective. However, it does not mean that you and each of your friends are free of *external* influences. Eliminating external influences can be difficult, but they can be reduced by sourcing perspectives of those not subject to the same environment you are, such as someone in a different culture, country, or age group. In fact, in some instances, the perspective of a young child might be your best source of a reality check.

Keep it simple: For us to reduce the errors in our take-home message, we need to work on reducing the internal and external influences on how we see and encode things, as well as minimizing errors such as assumptions and preconceived ideas. Finally, ensuring we have good sources of reality checks can help us hone our radar on how accurately we perceive and encode things.

The Takeaway

Life is an endless teacher. We can choose to listen to this teacher and improve, or we can ignore it and carry on making the same mistakes while forever shaking our fists at the world and laying blame at its feet.

By making sure we consider our take-home message and working at not allowing our emotions to blind us to what we could learn, we start to listen to this teacher. Too often, we forget to consider what lesson we are *choosing* to learn, and what we learn is due to reaction or emotion rather than careful consideration and active choice.

I don't believe we should disregard emotion; we should let it be part of our learning, but we should not allow it to be our only source of information on the experience. Be sure to step back, consider your levels of responsibility in any matter, be fair, kind, and compassionate to yourself, and consider what you are encoding for your future. Your take-home message will sculpt your future, perhaps a little, perhaps a lot, but the more you encode the same learning, the more you will come to believe it. So be careful what you choose to learn and where you learn it.

Final Thoughts

I hope that these four common patterns or factors have been presented in a way that can assist in identifying some of the underlying processes at play throughout our lives or the lives of those close to us. I'm a strong believer that the better we understand something, the more influence we have over it. Many of the clients I have worked with over the years have been very well-meaning and decent individuals who simply didn't understand why they faced the issues they did and how they may have been contributing to them. Those clients who had the courage and humility to face these things and accept their unwitting mistakes often went on to make changes for themselves, and consequently, their relationships with others and themselves greatly improved.

For anyone in a state of conflict with someone else, I highly recommend you consider the Blame-Responsibility Dynamic. It is something that I see on repeat when it comes to conflict or general relationships. In fact, the more problematic or conflictual a relationship is, the clearer this dynamic seems to be. For those of you facing constant frustration with your partners (or co-workers), consider who is blaming who, and who is or is not taking responsibility. Equally, for those raising children, be aware of how this dynamic can play out, and be sure to teach your child a healthy approach for their development. Save them the torment of being disliked due to a lack of personal responsibility. In my view, I would suggest that the Blame-Responsibility Dynamic is the measure of adulthood, and it's much easier to learn this in childhood than to change it in adulthood. If ever you want a clear example of an adult who failed to learn the impacts of this dynamic, simply go spend an evening with your local "Man-child."

CHAPTER 8 – FACTOR 4: THE TAKE-HOME MESSAGE

The Primary Pitfall and being aware of it is a strange juncture of becoming aware of complex human nature in adults and facing your own moral code. Unfortunately, we are often either shielded from the ills of the world or taught they do not exist, be it by a caring parent or a sculpted social engineering effort by one's culture, media, government, or other influencers. Every society or culture across history and the world will either subtly or overtly teach a set of morals or principles by which to live; religion is a good example of this, as is any subculture. These are not inherently bad or evil things; they are simply reality. What is important is that we are aware of this, as sadly, many seem to blindly follow without consideration of *who* is leading or *where* they are leading.

My hope with bringing the Primary Pitfall to light is that people will consider it when facing significant life moments but not be led to some belief that we have no common morals within our societies, cultures, or groups. If we can be aware there is a broad spectrum of human nature, and we can all inhabit certain and potentially different sections of this, then not only will we be less prone to be blindsided by others, but we can also protect those around us from bad actors. I might summarize the Primary Pitfall as the point where assumptions and naivety meet understanding and reality. My hope is that this can help keep our eyes open to identify the good and the bad actors that we come across throughout life.

The sense of shock, confusion, or pain that results from some decision in life can often be traced back to failing to understand the costs of a decision prior to having made it. I've seen and personally experienced the pain and suffering that can result from making a decision without being aware of its true and ultimate costs. Although we cannot ever be entirely across what any of our decisions will come to, I do believe that we can improve our odds for good decision-making if we are aware of what prevents us from doing so. If we can get some insight or separation from our emotions of the time and be aware of our deeper unconscious processes, then we can reduce our blind spots or at least interrupt a repeating pattern in life. Growing this awareness is not easy; however, it takes a great deal of humility to admit it and strength to combat it. It requires us to do what is hard, not easy. So, we must keep in mind that doing what is easy is often not what is best, and doing what is hard is often the path to growth or development of some sort. Knowing the costs can be a difficult task, as can choosing to pay or not pay certain costs, but with increased awareness, we are able to make more conscious decisions in our lives.

The take-home message is perhaps the most subtle of the four factors I've covered but by no means the least valuable. Too often, we go through life either not considering what something means or what we have learned from it or only do so when something has gone terribly wrong. On a mild scale, this is the case of only looking at the answers you got wrong on an exam or only doing that much if you happened to fail the exam. On a more impactful scale, we only stop to examine what went wrong in our marriage after it's over. Importantly, if we do not consider the take-home message actively, then we run the risk of simply reinforcing some childhood belief or general bias that likely grew out of someone else's inadequacy, inaccuracy, or fallacy.—the teacher who said you would amount to nothing, the drunk or absent parent who taught you that you were unlovable, the passing comment of a coach or aunt that you took to heart and unconsciously looked for evidence of everywhere you turned.

I have worked with countless clients suffering from debilitating anxiety who have a deeply entrenched belief that they are not good enough in some way or are unable to do something such as socialize or drive. Despite seeing thousands of such cases, I have yet to come across even one that was accurate in their belief. In fact, it is often the academically capable person who presents with paralyzing fear and believes they will fail an exam or the lovely, kind, considerate, and highly likable person who is petrified of not being socially accepted or approved of. Should any of these individuals be able to shift their mindsets from a "past belief" to a new one by being mindful of their take-home message, then not only would their anxiety reduce, but they would start to have a

CHAPTER 8 – FACTOR 4: THE TAKE-HOME MESSAGE

more accurate and healthy relationship with themselves and their future. Never underestimate the impact of how we encode a memory or what we choose to believe. These things will steer your life, so be very mindful of what self-talk you allow.

Each of these concepts ties together to provide specific ways of advancing through one's adult development. By being aware of them and implementing change, we can take a step towards more responsible adult living. This can lead us towards greater self-acceptance and much healthier relationships with those around us. With any luck, this can lead to a reduction in general life stress and anxiety and improved general mental health.

For those of you reading this book for yourselves or a loved one, my hope is that these four factors will help you better understand yourself or your loved one. I encourage you to approach any changes or improvements with kindness towards yourself and others, remembering that no one is intentionally trying to do a bad job in life. Often, we simply don't know what we're doing.

As for the therapists or budding psychologists out there, I hope that the content I've covered is received in the spirit it is intended and that it highlights important aspects that might otherwise be overlooked or forgotten. These factors are not a replacement for any therapeutic method, nor serve as a cure-all. However, by identifying if any of these factors are present in clients, we can help them gain a greater understanding of themselves, which not only aids their therapy but often simplifies it.

A common question I hear from my students is, "What should I look for in my clients?" My hope is that the discussions on anxiety and the four common factors can begin to guide you in the right direction or at least broaden your perspective beyond the formulaic processes of therapeutic methods like CBT, ACT, or other manualized approaches to treatment.

If the concepts raised in this book have piqued your interest, I highly recommend exploring the fields of psychodynamic or psychoanalytic psychology, as well as person-centered approaches. Key figures of the field, such as Carl Jung, developmental theorists like John Bowlby, Erik Erikson, and Jean Piaget, and human-centered therapists like Carl Rodgers, offer invaluable insights and are excellent starting points for further study.

Above all else, be kind to yourself as you factor in where you came from and how you can improve upon who you are today. We are all victims of our childhood and had no choice in what we were exposed to. We also have little influence on our development until we realize how we were shaped by our early experience, so keep this in mind when facing your less desirable sides.

As adults, we have a choice of what we do next. We all have the choice to take responsibility for ourselves and either choose to improve upon that or use it as a lifelong excuse for our poor behaviors and choices. Finding the courage to do this can be difficult at times, but no more so than continuing life as an under or poorly developed adult. The sooner we make a start, the sooner we see results, and the sooner we can come to the point of self-acceptance and long-term contentment, if not satisfaction.

References

Stinson, F. S., Dawson, D. A., Goldstein, R. B., Chou, S. P., Huang, B., Smith, S. M., ... & Grant, B. F. (2008). Prevalence, correlates, disability, and comorbidity of DSM-IV narcissistic personality disorder: Results from the Wave 2 National Epidemiologic Survey on Alcohol and Related Conditions. *Journal of Clinical Psychiatry*, 69(7), 1033-1045. https://doi.org/10.4088/jcp.v69n0701

www.ingramcontent.com/pod-product-compliance
Lightning Source LLC
Chambersburg PA
CBHW031148020426
42333CB00013B/564